JESUS SHOCK

PETER KREEFT

Be Bold. Be Catholic.®

JESUS SHOCK

Copyright © 2008 by Peter Kreeft
Published by Beacon Publishing
with permission from St. Augustine's Press

Printed in the United States of America. [1]

ISBN: 978-1-937509-17-0

Cover Design: Shawna Powell

Library of Congress Cataloging in Publication Data
Kreeft, Peter.
Jesus-shock / by Peter Kreeft.
p. cm.
Includes index.
1. Jesus Christ—Presence.
2. Jesus Christ—Person and offices.
3. Lord's Supper—Real presence. I. Title.
BT590.P75K74 2008
232—dc22   2008009137

Dynamic Catholic® and Be Bold. Be Catholic.®
and The Best Version of Yourself®are
registered trademarks of The Dynamic Catholic Institute.

For more information on this title
and other books and CDs available through
the Dynamic Catholic Book Program, please visit:
www.DynamicCatholic.com

The Dynamic Catholic Institute
5081 Olympic Blvd
Erlanger, Kentucky 41018
Phone: 1–859–980–7900
Email: info@DynamicCatholic.com

Contents

Dedication

To my father on earth, who introduced me to my Father in Heaven.

And to my Father in Heaven, who introduced me to my father on earth.

Part One: Seven Beginnings

Beginning #1
The Puzzling Question
This Book Answers

THIS BOOK HAS SEVEN beginnings. I don't call them introductions or prefaces to the book because they are beginnings of the book itself. They are all questions.

Nothing is more meaningless than an answer to a question that is never asked. Here, in two short pages, is the question this book answers. Everything else in the book is part of the answer.

The question is this: Why is Jesus the most controversial and the most embarrassing name in the world?

No one is embarrassed if you talk about Buddha, or Muhammad, or Moses. Neither Buddhists nor non-Buddhists are embarrassed to talk about Buddha. Why are almost all educated, non-fundamentalist Christians embarrassed to talk about Jesus to non-Christians, and why are almost all non-Christians embarrassed to hear such talk?

If you're not sure my assumption is true, test it, in any secular company, or mixed company, especially educated company. The name will fall with a thud, and produce sudden silence and embarrassment. You not only hear the embarrassment, you can feel it. The temperature drops. Or rises. It never stays the same.

You might answer that Christians are embarrassed not for themselves but for others: they are embarrassed only because they are sensitive to the embarrassment they know the name of Jesus will cause to non-Christians. But that only pushes the mystery back one step: why are non-Christians so embarrassed at this name? Why is "Jesus" the most non-neutral name in the world?

Jesus talk is like sex talk. There is no neutral language for sex. All our words about sex are either "sexy" or an attempt to avoid being "sexy." They are either (1) the ecstatic language of love, or (2) the gutter language of raunch, or (3) the tension-releasing language of the laugh (sex and religion are the two most popular subjects of jokes), or (4) the deliberately impersonal, scientific, and technological language of clinical medicine. And our words about Jesus are either (1) love-words, or (2) blasphemy words, or (3) jokes, or (4) impersonal, technical, theological words.

I'll bet you never realized this before: the perfect correlation between Jesus talk and sex talk. Why didn't you see it before? It's both obvious and interesting. Is it too close? Is it embarrassing? Why?

Jesus is a sword. He divides. You cannot be neutral about Him until you make a deliberate effort to thrust something away, something in your heart: either passionate attraction or passionate rejection of something, or at least deep embarrassment at something. Is it just at Christians? Is it at Christianity? Or is it at Christ?

Why is He history's greatest divider? Why is He the razor edge of the round world? What does He do to you, to put you on that edge, no matter who you are and no matter what you believe or don't believe?

Beginning #2:
What Is This Book About?

Reader: Why should I read this book? What is it about?

Author: It's about the difference Jesus makes.

Reader: The difference He makes to what?

Author: To everyone He meets.

Reader: But there are thousands of different answers to that question. That would require thousands of different books.

Author: No, only one. Because there is a single answer, a single phenomenon, which I call "Jesus-shock," and that phenomenon has been all but forgotten. And even when it is not forgotten, it has not been named. This book identifies it and names it.

Reader: I am skeptical. What new could be said about Jesus, after 2000 years?

Author: Everything. He makes all things new. Just watch. "Come and see."

Beginning #3:
A Self-Test, A Questionnaire

HERE IS A SELF-TEST. It helps you to know yourself and your philosophy of life, your "worldview." Don't worry about its connection with this book: that will come after the test.

Answer, as honestly and as concisely as you can, each of the following questions. Be sure you write your answers down in the blanks, rather than just thinking about them. You can deceive yourself about your thoughts very easily, but you cannot deceive yourself about what you make with your hands and see with your eyes.

First, ten personal questions, questions about persons:

1–3. Who do you think are the three greatest living persons in the world today?

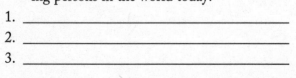

4. Who do you think is the most powerful person in the world today, whether for good or for evil? _____

5.–10. Name the person you turn to first for advice and help when you have problems in each of the following areas of your life:

5. mental health_____
6. marriage_____
7. money _____
8. sex _____
9. family _____
10. work, career _____

Next, some theological questions:

11. Why did God create the universe?

_____

12. How can we know God?

_____

13. What is God like?

_____

14. Why do you believe in life after death?_____

15. What is the secret of getting wisdom?

_____

16. How can a wicked person become righteous? _____

17. How can you become a saint?

_____

18. When you die and meet God and He asks you why He should let you into Heaven, what will you say?

_____

19. What is the Church?

_____

20. What is the solution to the problem of war?

_____

21. What did St. Paul know that you do not know that made him such an effective evangelist?

_____

22. Christianity seems to be just one religion among many in the world. How can this local, Western, Jewish, particular thing be for everyone, universally?

_____

23. What is Christianity? What does it preach, say, claim, or proclaim?

_____

Next, some philosophical questions:
24. What is truth?

_____

25. Define your way of life.

_____

26. Define "life."

_____

27. What is death?

_____

Next, some psychological questions:
28. What is the end, goal, and purpose of your life?_____

29. What is your solution to boredom?

_____

30. Define your true identity. Who are you?

_____

31. Why is your identity so mysterious?

_____

32. What is the best cure for loneliness?

_____

33. What can you do when you feel tired all the time?

_____

Finally, two questions to pull it all together:
34. What was the last command of the last apostle?

_____

35. What is the most frequently disobeyed Commandment?

The Point of the Test

After you write down your honest answers—*only* after you write down your honest answers—you should now grade yourself. By what standard? The New Testament. If you are a Christian, your answers should match. If they don't match, this means that you still have something to learn about being a Christian; and that means that perhaps you need this book.

Here are the New Testament's answers to all thirty-five questions, in boldface type. You can summarize all thirty-five answers in the same single five-letter word. It is "the name that is above every name" (Phil. 2:9), the name to which the angels beyond the universe and all the powers of the universe must bow (Phil. 2:10).

1.–3. *Who are the three greatest living persons?*
"Why do you seek the living among the dead?" **(Lk. 24:5)**

If you didn't say the Father, the Son, and the

Holy Spirit, why? Do you think God is impersonal? Do you think that only *human* persons are persons? Even if you thought that, why didn't you list Jesus? Do you really, deep down, think of Him as dead, not alive?

4. *Who is the most powerful person in the world today?*

"And Jesus said to them: all authority in heaven and earth has been given to me." (Mt. 28:18)

If you didn't answer "Jesus" for this question, you don't really believe what He told you in Mt. 28:18. And that's probably why you didn't answer "Jesus" to the next five questions too.

5.–10. *Who do you turn to to solve these problems in your life?*

"My God will supply all your needs according to his riches in glory in Christ Jesus." (Phil. 4:19)

"All" means all, not "some" or "only religious" or "only supernatural" or "only spiritual."

Of course He uses human instruments. But without Him, they have *no* power ("Without Me you can do nothing": Jn. 15:5), and without them He still has *all* power.

11. *Why did God create the universe?*

"All things were created through him [Christ] *and* *for him.***" (Col. 1:16)**

Jesus is not merely the universe's savior; He is the universe's purpose. The Incarnation was not a last-minute fix-it operation. And it was not undone in the Ascension. He is still incarnate, still with us. He is with us in different ways. He is with us through all material things, for He created them and He sanctified all matter by incarnating Himself in matter. He is with us more especially in the flesh of humanity. That is why "whatever you do to one of the least of these my brethren, you do to me." (Mt. 25:40)

And He is with us most completely in the Eucharist. That is why we can hear from everything in the universe an echo of the words we hear in the Mass: "This is My Body." Like Christ Himself, the Mass is not a mere fix-it operation but the key to the meaning of the universe. It is why God banged out the Big Bang.

12. *How can we know God?*

"No one has ever seen God; the only-begotten Son, who is in the bosom of the Father, he has made him known." (Jn. 1:18)

When anyone attains true knowledge of God, whether his name is Peter or Paul or Augustine or Aquinas or Moses or Socrates or Aristotle or Muhammad or Lao Tzu, that knowledge comes from Christ, the Logos, "the true light who enlightens every man who comes into the world." (Jn 1:9) He is the one and only Sun of God; every other being in God's Solar System is only a satellite, a planet, reflecting His light. The Solar System is a *system* only because it has a Center.

13. *What is God like?*
"He who has seen me has seen the Father." (Jn. 14:8–9)

That's it. There is nothing more. The Father is not Jesus plus x. God is love, and love holds nothing back, so God the Father holds nothing back in expressing Himself in God the Son. It's all in Colossians 1:15–20. Look it up.

14. *Why do you believe in life after death?*
"I am the resurrection and the life; he who believes in me, though he die, yet shall he live, and whoever lives and believes in me shall never die." (Jn. 11:26)

Death is not a philosophical problem but a live

one. Its solution is not a philosophical argument but a live person. The object of our hope is not the correctness of a human argument but the faithfulness of a divine Person.

15. *What is the secret of getting wisdom?*
16. *How can a wicked person become righteous?*
17. *How can you become a saint?*
18. *When you die and meet God and He asks you why He should let you into Heaven, what will you say?*
"Christ Jesus, whom God made our wisdom, our righteousness and sanctification and redemption." (I Cor. 1:30)

He is not merely the *source* or *cause* of our wisdom, our righteousness, our sanctification, and our redemption; He *is* our wisdom, our righteousness, our sanctification, and our redemption. We are shocked to find these abstractions incarnated and made concretely real in Jesus. But He is shocked to find Himself reduced to abstractions in us. Our weak faith actually shocks Jesus (see Mt. 8:11–12; Mk. 6:6; Mk. 14:33; Jn. 9:30).

19. *What is the Church?*
"the Church, which is his body, the fullness of him who fills all in all." (Eph. 1: 22–23)

It is an organism before it is an organization, and an incarnation before it is an institution. He is not its *boss*, He is its *head*—not as Bill Gates is the "head" of Microsoft but as that hairy ball between your shoulders is the head of your body. Your body *is* you. His body *is* He. When you feel threatened by the Church, listen to the One who speaks from beneath those humble, human appearances: "It is I; be not afraid."

The Church is not in the world; the world is in the Church as the setting is in the play. God made the universe in order to make saints, and the Church is "the communion of saints." The universe is God's saint-making machine, and the Church is its product.

20. *What is the solution to the problem of war?*
"Peace I give to you, my peace I leave with you. Not as the world gives do I give to you." (Jn. 14:27)

He *is* our peace. Nothing else has ever worked.

For everything else has tried to make peace, and to make compromises, with the world, the flesh, and the devil. But the only way to make peace with neighbor, self, and God is to make war on the world, the flesh, and the devil. That's what Jesus did.

21. *What did St. Paul know that you don't that made him such an effective evangelist?*

"I decided to know nothing among you except Jesus Christ." (I Cor. 2:2)

Less is more. Everything added to Jesus dilutes Him. All good theology, all authentic morality, all great liturgy is an unfolding of Jesus from within. All bad theology, morality, and liturgy are a diluting of Jesus. Evangelists like St. Paul who give people "Jesus only" change the world. For Jesus is irresistible. Evangelists who give people Jesus plus themselves do not change the world much. For human beings are resistible.

Mother Teresa was the most influential and admired Christian in the 20th century because she knew *less* than any other Christian did. Jesus was enough for her.

22. *Christianity seems to be just one religion among many in the world; how can this local, Western, Jewish, particular thing be for everyone, universally?*

"Here there cannot be Greek and Jew, circumcised and uncircumcised, barbarian, Scythian, slave, freeman, but Christ is all, and in all." (Col. 3:11)

Christianity = the story of the Gospel, the Incarnation, the Author becoming a character in the play. This Author is the Author of the whole play of human life, in fact the Author of the whole universe. He seems to be smaller than the play, since He is in it, by the Incarnation—in fact He is in it first as a tiny, one-celled zygote! But He is really infinitely bigger than the universe, since He is its Author.

23. *What is Christianity? What does it preach, or say, or claim, or proclaim?*

"this mystery, which is Christ in you, the hope of glory. Him we proclaim." (Col. 1:27–28)

The Christian *kerygma*, or proclamation, is the presence of a Person. If reduced to the shortest possible sentence, it would be: "Boo!"

24. *What is truth?*
25. *Define your way of life.*
26. *What is life?*

"I am the way, the truth, and the life." (Jn. 14:6)

Once again, abstractions acquire hands and feet and lips. Other teachers teach the way, the truth and the life, but He *is* the way, the truth, and the life. He is what they teach. That's why He does not write books. He does not point to a book because all books point to Him insofar as they are true.

27. *What is death?*

"For me to live is Christ, and to die is gain." (Phil. 1:21)

If your life is Christ, then your death will be only more of Christ, forever. If your life is only Christlessness, then your death will be only more Christlessness, forever. That's not fundamentalism, that's the law of non-contradiction.

28. *What is the end, goal, and purpose of your life?*

"until we all attain . . . to the knowledge of the Son of God, to mature manhood, to the measure of the stature of the fullness of Christ." (Eph. 4:13)

John Paul the Great loved to repeat this formula: Christ shows us not only who God is but also who we are, not only the meaning of God but also the meaning of man. The meaning of human life is to grow up, and to grow up means to become more like Christ.

29. *What is your solution to boredom?*

"If any man be in Christ, he is a new creature; old things are passed away, behold, all things are become new." (II Cor. 5:17)

"I have seen everything," said the bored philosopher. (Eccl. 1:14; 7:15) But he had not. He had not seen Christ. "There is nothing new under the sun," he said. (Eccl. 1:9) But there is: the Man who came from beyond the sun. Christ is the answer to the bored question: "What's new?" His answer is: "Behold, I make all things new." (Rev. 21:5)

30. *Define your true identity. Who are you?*
"I have been crucified with Christ; it is no longer I who live but Christ who lives in me." (Gal. 2:20)

The Cross crosses out the "I."

This is the secret of life: the self lives only by dying, finds its identity (and its happiness) only by self-forgetfulness, self-giving, self-sacrifice, *agape* love. Because that's what God is, that's what reality is, that's the way it is, that's the ultimate fact. "From the highest to the lowest, self exists to be given away, and only thus can it be found." (C.S. Lewis, *The Problem of Pain*, "Heaven") Every religion in the world knows some aspect of that ultimate secret. Christianity knows its ultimate foundation: that it is the life of the eternal Trinity.

31. *Why is your identity so mysterious?*
"For you have died, and your life is hidden with Christ in God." (Col. 3:3)

We are *supposed* to have an identity crisis. We are supposed to be living amid all the confusion and excitement of an old house being torn down and a new house being built in the very same place and time. We are caterpillars (Adams) in process of transformation into butterflies (Christs).

32. *What is the best cure for loneliness?*
"Behold, I am with you always, to the close of the age." (Mt. 28:20)

No one is ever alone. Christians know why, because they know Who.

33. *What can you do when you feel tired all the time?*
"Come unto me, all you who labor and are heavy laden, and I will give you rest." (Mt. 11:28)

Spiritual exhaustion is more devastating than physical exhaustion. And spiritual rest is more exhilarating than physical rest.

He gives you deepest rest even in the middle of exhaustion. When I thought my five-year-old daughter was going to die, I felt total emotional exhaustion, yet I knew there was an immovable anchor at the bottom of that stormy sea. It was He. It didn't calm the storm on the surface, but it held the boat fast.

34. *What was the last command of the last apostle?*

35. *What is the most frequently disobeyed Commandment?*

"Jesus Christ. This is the true God and eternal life. Little children, keep yourselves from idols." (I Jn. 5:20–21)

God put the Commandments into a deliberate order: first things first. For the Commandments are for us, for our needs, and the first thing we need is true life, eternal life; and that is found only in the true God. That's why worshipping false gods is so devastating: it's eating food that does not keep you alive.

The essential claim of Christianity is that "Jesus Christ . . . is the true God and eternal life." Idols are alternatives to Him, substitutes for Him. Today, idols are not made of wood, stone, or brass. They are made of money, sex, and power. But they are also made of subtler things. Some of these things are the things you wrote on the 35 blanks above.

What is the point of this exercise?

Jesus is the point. Everything comes to a point in Him.

The New Testament answers every one of

these thirty-five questions in the same way, with a single word: Jesus. Jesus is *"The* Word of God," God's single answer to all our questions. If you gave different answers, however good they may be, you need this book.

If you did not use the same single word the New Testament uses to answer all thirty-five questions, I suggest you pray the following prayer:

> The dearest idol I have known,
> Whate'er that idol be,
> Help me to tear it from Thy throne
> And worship only Thee.
>
> – William Cowper, 1772

Pascal would not have needed to read this book. He wrote: "Not only do we only know God through Jesus Christ, but we only know ourselves through Jesus Christ; we only know life and death through Jesus Christ. Apart from Jesus Christ we cannot know the meaning of our life, or our death, of God or of ourselves." (*Pensées*)

St. Thomas Aquinas would not have needed to read this book. Shortly before his death, another monk observed him in the middle of the night alone in the monastery chapel, prone on the floor, praying. A voice came from the lips of Christ on the crucifix: "You have written well of Me, Thomas. What will you have as your reward?" Thomas answered, with perfect wisdom, perfect humility, and perfect chutzpah: "Only Yourself, Lord."

This book tries to bring you a bit closer to the wisdom of Pascal and Aquinas.

Beginning #4:
Do You Need This Book?
Another Self-Test.

HERE IS A VERY simple test to identify your need for this book.

Read the following paragraph, from the greatest Christian writer of the 20th century. It is about the whole point of this book, what I have called "Jesus-shock." After you have read it, answer the single multiple-choice question that comes after it.

> Men are reluctant to pass over from the notion of an abstract . . . deity to the living God. I do not wonder. Here lies the deepest tap-root of Pantheism and of the objection to traditional imagery. It was hated not, at bottom, because it pictured Him as man but because it pictured Him as king, or even as warrior. The Pantheist's God does nothing, demands nothing. He is there if you wish for

Him, like a book on a shelf. He will not pursue you. There is no danger that at any time heaven and earth should flee away at His glance. If He were the truth, then we could really say that all the Christian images of kingship were a historical accident of which our religion ought to be purged. It is with a shock that we discover them to be indispensable. You have had a shock like that before, in connection with smaller matters—when the [fishing] line pulls at your hand, when something breathes beside you in the darkness. So here; the shock comes at the precise moment when the thrill of *life* is communicated to us along the clue we have been following. It is always shocking to meet life where we thought we were alone. "Look out!" we cry, "it's *alive*." And therefore this is the very point at which so many draw back—I would have done so myself if I could—and proceed no further with Christianity. An "impersonal God"—well and good. A subjective God of beauty, truth and goodness, inside our own heads—better still. A formless life-force surging through us, a vast power which we can tap—best of all. But God Himself, alive, pulling at the other end of the cord, perhaps approaching at an infinite speed, the hunter, king, husband—that is quite another matter.

There comes a moment when the children who have been playing at burglars hush suddenly: was that a *real* footstep in the hall? There comes a moment when people who have been dabbling in religion ("Man's search for God"!) suddenly draw back. Supposing we really found Him? We never meant it to come to *that!* Worse still, supposing He had found us?

So it is a sort of Rubicon. One goes across; or not. But if one does, there is no manner of security against miracles. One may be in for *anything*.

(C.S. Lewis, *Miracles*, ch. 11)

Now here is your multiple choice test on the passage above. Check the box that most accurately describes your reaction to it.

❑ Incomprehension. I simply have no idea what in the world this writer is talking about. This corresponds to nothing at all in my experience.

❑ Repulsion. I understand it all too well, and I will have nothing of it. I will run the other way as fast as I can to avoid this kind of religion.

❑ Wonder. I don't know whether I understand

it or not, since I have never experienced what he describes, but I wonder at it, with surprise and fascination, and I wonder *about* it, with curiosity.

❑ Longing. I understand it, and I long for it. I would love to be brought to the place this writer occupies.

❑ Recognition. I understand it, for I am there, where this writer is. This Lord is my Lord, and my soul's Lover, and I want to explore Him, and His presence, and our relationship forever.

Now, which category do you have to be in to read this book with profit?

Any one of them.

Beginning #5
A Third Self-Test

THIS TEST CONSISTS IN a single question:

What was the bitterest controversy of the Protestant Reformation, both between Protestants and Catholics and between different Protestant denominations, the one that had both sides calling the other not just heretics but devils?

Answer: It was *not* Justification by Faith, the hallmark of the Reformation, even though that question is about nothing less momentous than how to be saved, how to get to Heaven. It was *not* the relation between religion and politics, even though that was a matter of life or death (literally, on battlefields and at hangings). It was *not* about the sufficiency of the Bible, or the corruption in the Church, or the relation between the Bible and the Church. It was not about the Pope and the governance of the Church. It was *not* about Mary or saints or angels or Purgatory. It was *not* about the Incarnation or the Trinity or the Atonement.

It was about the Real Presence of Christ in the Eucharist.

It's not hard to understand why. Catholics accused Protestants of refusing Christ's most intimate and total invitation to union with Him that is possible in this life; of locking the doors of their bodies and their souls against the God-man who was knocking at those doors as truly, as really, as literally, and as completely, as when He roamed the streets of Israel in 30 A.D. and knocked at the door of a house. And Protestants accused Catholics of the most egregious idolatry in history, bowing down to bread and worshipping wine; of turning Christianity into paganism, as if by magic matter suddenly became God. Whoever is wrong about this is very, very importantly wrong indeed.

This book is about that question: not the theology of the Eucharist but the experience of Christ's Real Presence, which is the cause and explanation of "Jesus-shock."

Beginning #6
How This Book Was Born

THIS BOOK WAS BORN out of an intellectual barrenness. I was stuck in the middle of a long writer's block. So I put my stuck and empty mind in front of Christ in the Eucharist in the holy darkness of St. Mary's Chapel at Boston College and prayed wordlessly for a few minutes to the One who was there, until my lips formulated the question: What do *You* want me to write about?

The answer came immediately: "Me."

Instantly, resolution replaced confusion, and this book was conceived in the non-immaculate womb of my mind, when I said, "Let it be done to me according to Your word." I had written 40 books *for* Him, now I would write one *about* Him. (It took ten years and fifteen other books meanwhile for this book to feel right and jell and be finished. I couldn't push it. It was like a plant.)

This was radical progress: in my sixties, I finally remembered the superior wisdom I had had at age eight, when the best idea I ever had came to me.

My family was driving home from church on Sunday morning—I remember the exact spot, on Haledon Avenue and 8th Street in Prospect Park, New Jersey—when I suddenly said to my father, "Dad, all that stuff we learn in church and Sunday School—it's all really only one thing, isn't it?" Religion had seemed troublesome and complicated to me up until that moment, like the universe; but I thought I had finally found the "Theory of Everything," the Unified Field Theory in religion.

"Only one thing? What do you mean?" my father asked, skeptically.

"I mean, we only have to think about one thing and then everything else will be O.K., right? Just ask Jesus: What do *You* want me to do? And then do it."

My father turned to me with a surprised look. "You know, you're right, son, you're absolutely right." (My father was a wise man.)

I think it's been pretty much all downhill from there.

Of course, that idea came from the Holy

Spirit's wisdom, not mine. But if I could teach the world only one idea, that would be it. And if I could write only one book, this one would be it.

For *God* had only one idea, one Word: Jesus. Jesus is the total expression of God, the complete revelation of the Father, with nothing held back. "In him all the fullness of God was pleased to dwell." (Col. 1:19)

And as John Paul the Great loved to remind us, He is "the answer to which every human life is the question."

He is the Golden Key.

Beginning #7
The Golden Key

GEORGE MACDONALD'S "THE GOLDEN KEY" is my favorite fairy tale. (It was Tolkien's too.) Like all fairy tales, it is a quest story. But unlike other quest stories, it is not a quest for a key but for a door. The two protagonists, Mossy and Tangle, find a Golden Key at the very beginning. The story is their quest for the door or doors this key opens.

The story is an allegory. The Golden Key is Christ. This skeleton key opens all doors. And it has already been given to us, 2000 years ago. We have it.

But our story is not over, because our life is now the quest for the doors this Key opens. The questionnaire above showed thirty five of those doors. There are many more.

The allegory of the key and the lock is really backwards. For a key is a means to the end of solving the problem of the lock, opening the door. But Jesus is not a means to an end; He is the end, the final end and point and purpose and meaning and consummation of our lives.

So what happens when Christ the Golden Key opens the many locked doors of our lives is *not* that He is *added* to the picture, as a key is added to a lock. He is not an ingredient, not even the "key" ingredient, in the formula for our lives. He *is* "the life" as well as "the way." (Jn 14:6) Everything is an ingredient in Him. For He is the Logos, the Mind of God, the Author and Designer of all life. Shakespeare is not an ingredient in "Hamlet"!

Here is the way we usually look at Him:

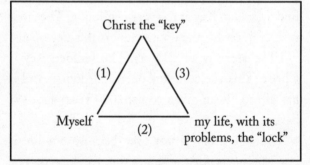

Thus we think of three relationships, symbolized by the three lines of the triangle:

(1) my faith, my relationship with Christ, my religion, my "spiritual life";

(2) my "secular" or "natural" life;

(3) Christ's solution to my problems.

But here is the right way to look at Him and at life. Here is the truth. Truth is defined by His mind, not mine. My mind sees things that way (the first diagram) but His mind sees things this way (the second diagram):

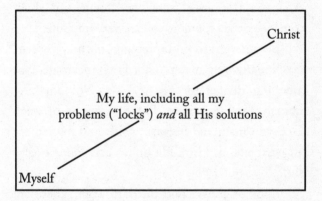

In all these parts of my life, I hear Him saying: "It is I; be not afraid." (Mt. 14:27) That present, living word from Him is "Jesus-shock." It is shock because we do not usually hear it, and when we do hear it, it comes out of the silence and shocks us, as the children in C.S. Lewis's parable are shocked by the sound of a real footstep in the hall when they were only playing at burglars.

We are all a little like the theologian who died

and was given the choice, by God, between going to Heaven or going to a lecture on Heaven, and he chose the lecture. We are all a little like Job's three friends who prate endlessly about God instead of talking *to* Him. In contrast, for Job God's very absence is a form of His presence. For Job prayed. You talk to someone present, not to someone absent. And you talk about someone absent, not about someone present, unless you are very impolite.

Because of His omnipresence, nothing is secular. Not anything material, for He is incarnate. Not anything divine, for He is God. Not anything human, for He is man. The separations between God and man, and between spirit and matter, are all overcome in Him. He unites *everything* except sin.

Look at the second diagram again: there are not three lines, but only one. Everything is a relationship with Him. Everything is a highway on which run the trucks of interworld commerce between God and man. Everything is a Jacob's Ladder on which the angels ascend and descend. He comes to us and we go to Him: that is the meaning of life. Life is a tube, open at both ends, through which we communicate and meet. The universe is a big cell phone to God.

Even the image of the Golden Key fails, for a key is the solution to the problem of opening a door. But Christ is not, ultimately, our *solution*. (Is your lover your "solution"?) He is our divine Lover and Lord. All the "problems" of life are part of His marriage to us, His lovemaking, His foreplay. As Francis Thompson wrote in his classic poem "The Hound of Heaven," "Is my gloom, after all, shade of His hand outstretched caressingly?"

All things in life must be that, because He is not relative to them, they are relative to Him. *Everything* is, for He is God, and God is the absolute.

He is not the solution to our problems; He is the giver of our problems. Our problems are His tasks and our opportunities, His teaching and our education, His will and our sanctification. Whether they are as small as a dropped earring or as large as a death or (worse) a divorce, everything is somewhere on that love-line that runs from Him to us. He is our Universal Other, the One we are always in dialog with, the One pulling at the other end of the line. Whether we see it or not, whether we believe it or not, we always struggle with Him, not with our problems, our lives, our deaths, our friends, or our families. They are on the line with us; He is the One at the end of the line. Do you have a child who is dead, or who has done something awful, or who is in terrible trouble? (No problem, no "locked door," can be bigger than that for a parent.) Christ is not a mere means to the end of solving your problem and relieving your sorrow. Your problem, however big it is (or however small), is His wise and loving will to you, even though it may not *look* wise or loving. It is His deliberate permissive will. And your response to it is your response to Him.

And when this absolute God steps into our world of relativities, full of problems and ignorances and sins, we have a shock like no other shock.

Part Two: The Data: Jesus-Shock

AT THE END OF my book *Socrates Meets Jesus*, Socrates asks an embarrassing question to his fellow students at Harvard Divinity School. He has found himself there somehow, 2400 years forward and 3500 miles westward, and has thought his way into Christianity simply by asking honest Socratic questions of his Modernist professors and confused fellow students, and not giving up until he finds the truth. But Socrates met Jesus at Harvard not just as a dead historical figure but as a living presence (the title of the chapter is: "Look Out: It's Alive!"), and his embarrassing question now is this: "Where are all the Christians?" Surely at least some people at this divinity school at the heart of Christendom must be Christians; why are they all under cover?

Socrates' words are: "If you are all Christians, if some of you are Christians, if any of you are Christians—how could your life be the same? How could you look the same, talk the same, think the same? . . . How could your life be so bland if this incredible thing is true?"

If Christianity is true, this changes *everything*. Christ's very last words to us in scripture were: "Behold, I make all things new." (Rev. 21:5) I hope you remember that most moving line in the most moving movie ever made, *The Passion of the Christ*, when Christ turns to His mother on the way to Calvary, explaining what He is doing and why He is doing it, explaining the need for the Cross and the blood and the agony: "See, Mother, I make all things new." I hope you remember that line with your tear ducts, which connect to the heart, as well as with your ears, which connect to the brain.

Christ changed every human being he ever met. In fact, He changed history, splitting it open like a coconut and inserting eternity into the split between B.C. and A.D. If anyone claims to have met Him without being changed, he has not met Him at all. When you touch Him, you touch lightning. Socrates is puzzled because he is looking for the burn marks.

Boredom

"Shocking" is the opposite of "boring." I think Jesus

is the only man in history who never bored anyone.
I think this is an empirical fact, not just a truth of
faith. It is one of the reasons for believing His central claim, and Christianity's central claim, that He
is literally God in the flesh. That is, of course, the
ultimate reason for the shock, and for the unique-
ness of the shock: it is like the shock of Macbeth
meeting not Banquo's ghost but Shakespeare; like
Frodo meeting not Gandalf but Tolkien.

The Greek word used to describe everyone's
reaction to him is *thauma*, "wonder." That was the
reaction of His enemies, who killed Him; of His
disciples, who worshipped Him; and even of
agnostics, who went away shaking their heads and
muttering "No man ever spoke like this man," and
knowing that if He didn't stop being what He was
and saying what He said, then eventually they
would have to side with either His killers or His
worshippers. For "Jesus-shock" breaks your heart in
two and forces you to choose which half of your
heart you will follow.

Boredom is one of our major psychological
problems today, though few of our "experts"
acknowledge this. I suspect that boredom is the
primary cause of violence and war. No one is bored
while they are killing someone else, or planning to.

Do you remember how *interesting* the TV news suddenly became when we started our last little war? Haven't you ever wondered how much of the psychological roots of war come from boredom? Can't you see that bored little bunch of ghostly children sitting around in the cellar of your unconscious looking for trouble? "Hey, yesterday sucked. What shall we do tomorrow?" "I know. Let's dress up in funny uniforms and get guns and find a big field and go out and kill each other." "Yay! What a great idea!"

We all know the harm boredom does if we have kids. The single most effective way to make them behave is to keep them interested. This is the single most practical principle of child management: kids will always get into trouble when they are bored.

Ah, but adults are only large kids, once you see through the transparent layers of socialization. Like kids, if we are to have any hope of improving their behavior, we first of all have to get their attention.

Promiscuous sex is another great boredom-reliever. Our culture, like late Rome's, is saturated with sex and violence because it is saturated with boredom.

Habitual boredom, boredom not with a specific task like chopping wood ten hours a day but with everything, boredom that is like the sky, spread over everything, not only leads to sin; it *is* a sin. The medievals called it "sloth," one of the Seven Deadly Sins. Sloth is not simply laziness. In fact, it does not necessarily imply any physical laziness at all. It means the passivity and inactivity of the will and the desires even in the presence of the true good. It is the soul's refusal to eat its food. Violence is spiritual junk food, and boredom is spiritual anorexia.

Where do we find sloth? Go to your nearest Sunday morning church service, Protestant or Catholic. Then go to your nearest athletic field, amateur or professional. Compare the interest, the passion, the energy, the investment of the heart in those two places. How much soul-stuff, how much of the self, rubs off in those two places? Full disclosure here: I'm a big God fan but most of the time I'm an even bigger Red Sox fan. I make more noise about beating the Damnyankees than about beating the Devil. I'm an idiot. That's one of the meanings of Original Sin.

Don't we know what's going on in church? Don't we know that we're attending a meeting of spies plotting a revolution against the Prince of This World? Don't we know the great Lion of the Tribe of Judah, who sneaks into our churches in disguise to meet us there? Apparently not. If we did, Annie Dillard would not need to write these words:

> Why do people in churches seem like cheerful, brainless tourists on a packaged tour of the Absolute? . . . Does anyone have the foggiest idea what sort of Power we so blandly invoke? . . . The churches are children playing on the floor with chemistry sets, mixing up a batch of TNT to kill a Sunday morning. It is madness to wear ladies' straw hats and velvet hats to church; we should be wearing crash helmets. Ushers should issue life preservers and signal flares; they should lash us to our pews. For the sleeping god may wake some day [and] draw us out to where we can never return. ("An Expedition to the Pole")

Why are we bored? What's missing?

It's not pleasure. We moderns are inveterate and successful hedonists. But no amount of pleasure satisfies us if it's boring. The most total opposite of pleasure is not pain but boredom, for we are willing to risk pain to make a boring life interesting. That's why we find war interesting, and also its civilized substitutes, sports and gambling, both of which are ritualized risk. That's also why the rich blow their brains out at an alarming rate, more than the poor do: because a lot of money makes life predictable and controllable and therefore boring. The unsurprising life is not worth living.

What is the opposite of boredom? Not pleasure, not even happiness, but joy. Joy always includes surprise, sometimes even shock. Joy's opposites—rage, outrage, horror, and terror—are also shocks. Those who meet Jesus always experience either joy or its opposites, either foretastes of Heaven or foretastes of Hell. Not everyone who meets Jesus is pleased, and not everyone is happy, but everyone is shocked.

Preaching is usually boring. Jesus does not usually preach. What does He do? He dances. Ultimately, He dances on His own grave. He rises from the dead not just on Easter Sunday but every day forever after that, like a jack-in-the-box. The Bible is a pop-up book. To put the point in duller, less symbolic language, Jesus keeps bursting asunder all our comfortable categories and keeps transcending all our feeble expectations. He is "full of grace and truth," and I think "grace" includes not just something morally good but also aesthetically good; not just "gift" but also "style." He is full of the grace of a Chopin nocturne, the grace of a Michael Jordan slam-dunk. He is God's supreme surprise.

Everything God does is a surprise. First, creation. There is no need for this. It is an utter superfluity. No pagan ever conceived the idea of the creation of all being out of nothing. When the Greek philosophers first heard of the idea, from Jews and Christians, and when they understood what it meant—not merely imposing new form on old matter but imposing existence on nonexistence—they thought the idea insane. For in creation, the God who is everything and needs nothing acts as if He needs everything. He comes out of Himself and creates a universe that is infinitely less than Himself and yet real, beings that are not Being Itself, real things that are really other than Reality Himself, thus shocking all pantheists down through the ages. We must understand how reasonable pantheism is: how can there be anything other than Being? Pantheism has always tempted rationalistic philosophers. But God is not reasonable, in any human, expected sense. It is closer to the truth to say that God is crazy than that God is reasonable. I suspect God merely smiles when someone calls him crazy, but shakes His head and frowns when someone calls Him reasonable.

And He creates not only matter but also angels, finite spiritual persons, other selves than Him. How can there be more than one "I"? That's even more unreasonable. Hindus and Buddhists are not crazy mystics; their metaphysics is perfectly reasonable. Hinduism says there is only one "I," Brahman; and Buddhism says there are none. But the Bible says there are billions!

Creating other spirits was crazy enough, but then He went on to create us: spirits that are also animals: angels that breathe and breed, organisms that think, mortal spirits, immortal animals. Like apes, we breed, sleep, and die. Yet like God we say, "I am." We are ontological oxymorons. The very word "oxymoron" is a providential joke, for we are animals like oxen and also spiritual morons, for sin is the stupidest thing imaginable. (It's so stupid that a rationalist like Plato found it literally unimaginable. He argued, very reasonably, that all evil was due to ignorance, that bad people simply don't know or realize that the happiness we all seek lies only in the life of goodness that they shun. How reasonable this idea is! But we all know from experience that it's not true.)

There's much more to God's craziness. He then went on to give these spiritual oxymorons, these "rational animals," free will and let them choose between Himself and Satan, Heaven and Hell, light and darkness, life and death. It is no charade: if we choose the Enemy, He lets us do it, and respects our freedom—forever. How can He act so *dangerously*? We wish He didn't. We wish He had put up snake fences around Eden.

So He let us make the most moronic choice in history, buying the Devil's apple advertisement. (By the way, if you get mad at your Mac laptop and wonder who designed this demonic device, notice the manufacturer's icon on top: an apple with a bite out of it.) So what did God do next? The craziest thing of all, the deed no sage, no saint, no philosopher, no mystic, no man, no angel, and no devil ever even dreamed of: He became a human zygote, fetus, baby, boy, teenager, man, and then corpse. To do this, He first sent His angel to meekly wait for a girl's consent to be His mother. God is such a gentlemen that He asked *permission* from His mother to be born! And God Almighty, infinite Spirit, the Second Person of the eternal Trinity, acquired a set of animal organs—forever. (For the

Ascension was not the undoing of the Incarnation.)

And then He gave Himself to our mouths and our stomachs as well as to our souls. That thing that looks like a little piece of bread—that's Him. I certainly sympathize with most Protestants, who do not believe that. It is nearly unbelievable. The priest puts God into your left hand, and you pick up God Almighty with your right thumb and forefinger and you swallow God Almighty, and He falls into your stomach. That is crazy—as crazy as the Incarnation.

This is 99.9999999999 percent unbelievable. Like the Incarnation. This baby who can't even speak until his parents teach him, this man who has nerve endings all over his body and gets hungry and tired and bloody and gets nailed to a cross and *dies*—that is the "holy God, holy strong one, holy immortal one," the eternal Word of the eternal Creator Who spoke all time and space and matter into being.

How can we believe this? Only because He Himself gives us the grace to believe it. Not only is the fact a miracle, our faith in it is also a miracle. It is a miracle that an honest and intelligent

Christian believes a truth that is nearly unbelievable. There is no miracle in dishonest faith, fake faith; nor in unintelligent faith, stupid faith, misunderstood faith, which confuses Christianity with something easily believable, like "God exists and Jesus is nice and we ought to love one another." But honest and intelligent faith in Christianity is literally a miracle. "Faith is a gift of God." God gives us not only the truth but also the ability to believe it; not only the new thing to see but also the new eye to see it with.

For how could we ever believe such a thing all by ourselves unless we were deranged? Try to imagine approaching any pious and intelligent Old Testament Jew with the Nicene Creed and expecting him to believe it. And yet, once believed, it is the most beautiful and precious thought ever conceived. We could never have impregnated our own mental wombs with this thought. For, as Kierkegaard says (in *Philosophical Fragments*, end of ch. 2), although it is possible that foolish little men might believe God was as foolish and as little as they were (thus pagan polytheistic mythology), or that they were as great and wise as God was (thus pantheistic mysticism), how was it possible that anyone would think that God would love man; that the God who needed nothing would act as if He needed man; that the blessed God Himself, the perfect One, would care so much for man that He would become man and let Himself be murdered by man in order to save man? If God gave no sign, how could we ever suspect that? It is inconceivable, incredible, impossible, and unimaginable. It's certainly not boring.

J.B. Phillips wrote a good book with a great title: "Your God Is Too Small." Someone should write a book entitled "Your God Is Too Boring." Since Jesus was the only man in history who never bored anyone, it follows that if your Jesus is boring, your Jesus is not the real Jesus. If it's a tame lion, it's not Aslan.

What did we do with this iron ball in the pit of the stomach that we could neither digest nor disgorge? In response to this divine miracle, man has produced an almost equally astonishing miracle. As Jesus turned water into wine, we have turned wine back into water, turned the intoxicating wine of the Gospel into a mushy grape jelly. He came to light a fire, and we have found a way to water it down. He came to shock us, and we have channeled the shock away through lightening rods called churches, or rather churchiness. He came to

spread his good infection, and we have found anti-
dotes. As the antidote for smallpox is cowpox; as
the antidote for a strong infection is a weak infection of the same germs, a weak infection that elicits antibodies to fight the strong infection; so the
antidote for potent religion is pallid religion. The
antidote for Christ is "Christian stuff." The antidote for his noun is our adjective.

No book is more fascinating than the Bible.
And no books are less fascinating than most of our
commentaries on the Bible. Nothing is more formidable and unconquerable than the Church Militant.
But nothing is more sleepy and sheepish than the
Church Mumbling. Christ's words roused His enemies to murder and His friends to martyrdom. Our
words reassure both sides and send them to sleep.
He put the world in a daze. We put it in a doze.

Thomas Day wrote a perceptive and funny
book called *Why Catholics Can't Sing*, but he missed
the main reason: we don't sing about our religion
because we're bored with it. Modernist Catholics
don't sing because they have nothing to sing about.
But faithful Catholics have something to sing
about, and therefore they do sing. They sing in very
different styles, some of them musically magnifi-
cent and some musically abominable, so style isn't

the reason they sing. They sing because they have met Jesus Christ. When you meet Him, you can't *not* sing, even if your voice is the voice of a crow.

Napoleon's soldiers sang the "Marseillaise" with gusto not because they were great singers but because they had great faith and love—for France and for Napoleon. Luther won Germany for his Reformation by his hymns, not by his theology. Southern Black slaves sang great spirituals because they had great faith and hope. Their right foot was already in Heaven while their left foot was on earth. It is as natural for the lover to sing as for the fire to burn. Only where faith and hope and love are weak, is song weak.

Find a parish that sings. Better yet, make your parish a parish that sings.

Beauty

Why is our faith and hope and love so pallid and weak and boring? Because it is not sensitive to beauty.

Beauty is one of the three foods of the soul, the three most vital human needs, along with Truth and Goodness. These are the three things we all want infinitely and absolutely. They are the three attributes of God that our very nature tells us about. They are the three ideals that raise us above the animals. They are also the three personality traits of Jesus in the Gospels that stunned everyone: His hard, practical wisdom; His warm, compassionate love; and His fascinating creativity and unpredictability. He was not only true and good, He was beautiful.

Christians have succeeded, and are still succeeding today, quite famously in the first of these two areas. Christian philosophy is the most intelligent of philosophies, and Christian morality is the most holy of moralities. But Christianity no longer produces the world's most beautiful and arresting art. Modern man is rejecting Christianity not because it looks stupid or wicked but because it looks boring: dull, hokey, embarrassing, "square," sissified, bland, repressive, platitudinous, preachy, dreary, "weary, stale, flat and unprofitable." Its pictures are no longer moving pictures. They do not move hearts. The secular media make the magic now.

This is a far more serious problem than most Christians think. Few Christians go into media or the arts today, or see it as a primary apostolate or mission field or battlefield. But it is. It's the part of the battlefield where we lost the world, and it's the place where we'll have to win it back.

The field is ripe for harvesting. Our world is rich, efficient, powerful, clever, knowledgeable—and ugly. We live in strip malls and hide beauty away in museums, instead of living in the museums and hiding away the ugliness. Look how we use the word "progress." When you hear the words "Oh, well, you can't stop progress," you can be quite certain that something beautiful has just been destroyed. Our culture has filled our heads but emptied our hearts, stuffed our wallets but starved our wonder. It has fed our thirst for facts but not for meaning or mystery. It produces "nice" people, not heroes.

Beauty, and the love and wonder and fascination it elicits, is an essential human need. It is not an ornament. But it is not only neglected by the masses, it is actively hated, feared, and attacked by the secular artistic community. The National Endowment for the Arts funds many diverse projects, but almost all of them have one thing in common: a hatred of beauty, a snobbish contempt for ordinary human nature and ordinary people's aesthetic hunger. They are on a holy war against the Holy Land of Beauty.

The anti-beauty jihadists are succeeding largely because we are failing to realize how important this battlefield is. It is not icing on the cake; it is one of the three layers of the cake. It is the child of the marriage of truth and goodness. It is "the splendor of truth" (to quote John Paul the Great's great title) that attracts us to truth, and it is "the beauty of holiness" (Psalm 29:2) that attracts us to holiness. Beauty is one of the things God is. It is "the glory of the Lord" (to use von Balthasar's title), the "divine Beauty ancient yet ever new" that won Augustine's restless heart. Beauty is a magnet, and our souls are iron filings, and when we sense beauty, we speed home.

Beauty relieves boredom because beauty is the object of love. Beauty turns our head whenever we see it because it turns our heart. The heart is like a woman, and the head is like a man, and although man is the head of woman, woman is the heart of man, and she turns man's head because she turns his heart.

We have never seen anything under the sun more beautiful than Christ. Nothing is more beautiful than a saint because a saint is a little Christ. A saint is more than a moralist. A moralist is a bore. Even Socrates is a bore compared to Saint Francis, because Socrates loved the moral law, but Saint

Francis loved the One behind the law. The saint is beautiful because the saint has penetrated to the Source of all beauty.

No story is more beautiful than the Gospel, "the greatest story ever told" (Tolkien says "There is no story men would rather believe was true"), even though it is a story full of pain and nails and hate and blood and sin and murder and betrayal and forsakenness and unimaginable agony and death. It is the story of what happens to the most beautiful thing, Perfect Love, when it enters our world: it comes to a Cross, to the crossroad between good and evil. T.S. Eliot called the Gospel "the idea of some infinitely gentle, infinitely suffering Thing." All our most beautiful stories are like the Gospel: they are tragedies first, and then comedies; they are crosses and then crowns. They are crosses because they are conflicts between good and evil. That is the fundamental plot of every great story. To say "that story is beautiful" means "that story resembles the Gospel."

If you are bored by the Gospel, that puts no black eye on the Gospel, but on you. Most likely, it means you have never listened to it. You must have heard it, but hearing is far from the same thing as listening—as you know when you try to talk to a "friend" who hears you but does not *listen*. You listen to music, but not to muzak.

Not all who listen, believe. If you call the Gospel a crazy fairy tale, a far-too-good-to-be-true myth, an insane extension of wishful thinking, or even a blasphemous lie, I will respect you and argue with you. But if you call it a platitude, I can only pity you, for that means you have never listened to it.

Christ's beauty is a beauty that breaks our hearts. It is "no beauty we could desire" unless our hearts break first. Deep truth heals your mind, and deep goodness heals your will, but deep beauty wounds your heart. Beauty hurts.

The most beautiful works of art in human history came from Christians. That was no accident. The connection between art and Christ is like the connection between sunlight and the sun. It is, in fact, the connection between Sonlight and the Son. It is a million points of light from the Light of the World, reflections of the Sun of God in the mirror of the waters of earth. When we listen; when we have the sanity to be still; when we do the most creative thing we can ever do with our minds, namely shut up and enter the holy silence; we find

Someone there who has been leading us beside those still waters, restoring our souls. The silence is not empty; it is full, like the silence in the eyes of a watching lion.

That is the explanation for the Gothic cathedrals of the Middle Ages. They were technological miracles, far ahead of their time, like the American moon rockets of the sixties. In fact, they were very much like moon rockets: heavy matter taught to fly like angels. Their flying buttresses looked a lot like rocket fins. When you look at the cathedral of Notre Dame, you are amazed that it has remained on its earthly launching pad so long. If you saw the whole massive structure suddenly blasting off from earth and ascending to Heaven in front of your eyes, you would say, "Of course. I knew it would come to that eventually." These cathedrals have been called "sermons in stones," but they are more than that: they are spirit in stone, angels in stone. Christ would not perform the miracle of turning stones into bread, but Christians performed the miracle of turning stones into angels.

What in the world explains these miracles? Nothing in the world. That's what makes them miracles. Christ alone explains those cathedrals. Stonemasons did not build them; faith built them.

His Real Presence built them, and His real presence was worshipped in them. They were built not to house man worshipping, but Christ worshipped. They were *His* houses; that's why they had to be better than man could possibly do. They had to be transgressions of the possible and imports of the impossible. Like the Cross. They were built in the shape of a cross because they were built by the crazy love of men for the Christ whose crazy love for men had brought Him to the Cross. They were the most beautiful buildings ever seen on earth because He lived and loved and acted in them, and He was the most beautiful thing ever seen on earth.

It is always our hearts that accept the Gospel first. The beauty-hungering heart always leads the truth-hungering head. It is the *beauty* of truth and the *beauty* of goodness that attracts us, not the mere correctness of them. The heart detects them first. The heat from a melting heart has to warm the frozen mind and will. And only the hardest heart can look without melting at that face on the Cross, knowing Whose face it is there, what He is doing there, what love moved Him to go there, and whose sins sent Him there.

The world was converted by the Gospel

because the Gospel is the beautiful love story of God's crazy love for man. The story of the world's conversion to this love story is also a love story: it is the story of man's love for this crazy God. We were not converted by the reasonableness of the story. The story is not reasonable! It would be far more reasonable for a man to love the rebellious ants in his pet ant farm so much that he became an ant and let the rebel ants torture him to death in order to save the ants from their sins. We sinned for no reason but an incomprehensible lack of love, and He saved us for no reason but an incomprehensible excess of love. Everything in the story is crazy, nothing is reasonable, nothing is expected, nothing is boring, and everything is beautiful.

How can our response to such beauty be boring instead of beautiful? How can we ossify and mummify the Living One? How did we invent the spiritual taxidermy that turns Christ the Tiger into a toy to cuddle and sell? Far better to shout, "Crucify him!" than to mumble comfortably, "Isn't he nice?" He is not Christ the Kitten but Christ the King, Christ the Tiger, Christ the Lion. And when you hear this lion roar, even if you believe it is only a myth, "a midsummer night's dream," you can't *not* say, with the good duke, "Let him roar again!"

Adoration

Watch how the wildness of man's love for this wild lover of man blows away boredom in the Gospel:

> And while he was at Bethany in the house of Simon the leper, as he sat at table, a woman came with an alabaster jar of ointment of pure nard, very costly, and she broke the jar and poured it over his head. But there were some there who said to themselves indignantly, "Why was the ointment thus wasted? For this ointment might have been sold for more than three hundred denarii [a year's wages] and given to the poor." And they reproached her. But Jesus said, "Let her alone; why do you trouble her? She has done a beautiful thing to me. For you always have the poor with you, and whenever you will, you can do good to them; but you will not always have me. She has done what she could; she has anointed my body beforehand for burying. And truly I say to you, wherever the gospel is preached in the whole world, what she has done will be told in memory of her." Then Judas Iscariot, who was one of the twelve, went to the chief priests in order to betray him. (Mark 14:3–10)

Though the New Testament does not explicitly say so, the traditional interpretation identifies this woman as Mary Magdalene. Imagine: a former prostitute adoring Jesus! Imagine: a year's wages (and remember how those wages had been earned!) "wasted" on a single bottle of perfume, and then the perfume "wasted" by spilling it all out at once on His dirty hair! You need not be Judas Iscariot to protest this. You need only be prudent and reasonable. This money could have saved a dozen families from poverty.

Now imagine another scene, 1500 years later. Imagine a tortured but pious and brilliant homosexual artist commissioned by the Pope himself to design the central church in all Christendom for the rest of time. Imagine half the world's gold wasted on this church when half the world is in poverty. You see? It's the same story. It continues. And we continue to be tempted to side with Judas instead of Jesus.

We know the end of *Judas's* story: we know the two deeds of death he was responsible for, first Christ's and then his own, the two most important people in the world to him, the only two from whom he could never escape, in time or in eternity. His physical suicide came only after his spiritual suicide, which happened in this Gospel story. What prompted him to betray Jesus *then?* What did Mary Magdalene do that was so outrageous that Judas responded to it by choosing damnation?

The answer, in one word, is adoration. That is the definitive and eternal answer to the problem of boredom, because that is the business of Heaven. Everything smaller than Heaven bores us because only Heaven is bigger than our hearts. And if we turn away from adoration in disgust, as Judas did, for any reason whatsoever, however prudent, then we turn from *Him* and from Heaven. That's what Michal did when David danced in adoration before God's Ark. (2 Sam. 6:16)

Adoration is love unlimited, love squared, love raised to infinity by the exponent of love itself. Adoration is the mountain without a summit, the Jacob's Ladder that extends into the sky forever. Only God may be adored, because only God is unlimited goodness, truth, and beauty, and thus only God deserves unlimited love. Our very "first and greatest commandment" is to love Him with all our heart, soul, mind, and strength. (Mk. 12:30) If we give *that* love to any creature, even our spouse, we commit adultery against God. That is what idolatry is: spiritual adultery. Alas, we all commit spiritual adultery—with ourselves. We are commanded to love our neighbor only "as ourselves"—and we are certainly not to adore our-selves. That is why we are not to adore our neigh-bor. We must not treat anyone, whether ourselves or our neighbors, as God, by loving them with our *whole* heart. And we are certainly not to give our whole heart to *stuff.* Even stupider is to give our whole heart to money, which is only stuff to exchange for stuff. And that's what Judas did.

When she was a prostitute, Mary Magdalene did not love herself, or God, or the men she seduced. She loved the stuff she bought with the money, and she loved the money she bought with her body, and she loved her body only because it could buy the men and their money and the stuff—like expensive perfume. Then she exchanged autonomy for adoration, and gave all her soul and all her body and all her life and all her money and all her stuff to Christ. That perfume was the stuff and the money and the men and the prostitution and her life and her heart, all rolled into one ball. That's the ball she gave to Christ, like a good dog, instead of holding on to it, like a bad dog. And that is the secret of joy. We can learn it even from our dogs. Christ teaches us joy through our dogs, but we don't listen.

Plotting and planning and buying and selling

are boring. Economics is "the grey science," even though it's perfectly honorable and necessary. But giving it all away is not boring. The rich fop Francis of Assisi was bored all his life—until he fell in love with Christ and gave all his stuff away and became the troubadour of Lady Poverty. St. Paul used a striking word for this "stuff"—that is, for everything else in the world except Christ—when he called it *skubala* in Philippians 3:8–10. It is a four-letter word in English, and it begins with an "s". The strong, bold, honest, and literal King James Bible translators let us know what it meant: "dung."

But this was expensive dung. To the rest of the world, Paul's *skubala* didn't stink. Paul had known the very best the world could offer: Roman citizenship, education at the feet of Gamaliel, "the Light of Israel," prestige and power among both Jews and Romans. He even knew moral "success" by the standards of the most morally rigorous sect of the most morally rigorous religion (Judaism) in the world: he was "a Pharisee of the Pharisees; as touching the law, blameless." And he laid all this stuff at the feet of Christ and called it *skubala*. Why? For the same reason Dante could see the most beautiful woman in the world as a bagel compared with Beatrice: because love gives you eyes.

Love is reasonable in the deepest sense, and therefore unreasonable in the normal sense. The deepest sense of "reason" is the rule of the three R's: "right response to reality." The normal, shallower sense of "reason" is "practical prudence." That's fine for finitude, but infinity demands insanity. The crazy love of a saint is reasonable because it is the only right response to the reality of infinity. It is reasonable to love the Absolute absolutely for the same reason it is reasonable to love the relative relatively. And it is just as unreasonable to love the Absolute and the Infinite with a relative and finite love, that is, to be prudent and practical like Judas in the presence of Christ, as it is to love the relative and the finite with an idolatrously absolute and infinite love. It is just as crazy *not* to be crazy about Christ as it is to be crazy about anything else. He is "not Yes *and* No but pure Yes" (I Corinthians 1:19), and therefore the saint loves Him with a pure Yes.

This is the heart and essence of true religion. And it is madness by the world's standards. (Freud was honest enough to call it that, literally.) The madness of Mary's adoration moved Judas to the madness of self-damnation. John's Gospel notes that Satan entered Judas also when Judas witnessed two other similarly mad acts of love: first, Christ washing His disciples' feet, and then Christ giving them His own body and blood in the first Eucharist in the Upper Room. (Jn. 13:1–30) Judas saw the purest love ever seen on earth and could not endure the sight, so he put out his own eyes. He saw Heaven on earth and could not endure it, and that non-endurance is the only reason why there is Hell.

On another occasion, we see the same fanatic love in another Mary provoking a little bit of the same "reasonable" prudence in Martha as we saw in Judas. But unlike Judas, Martha later listened and learned.

> Now as they went on their way, he entered a village; and a woman named Martha received him into her house. And she had a sister called Mary, who sat at the Lord's feet and listened to his teaching. But Martha was distracted with much serving; and she went to him and said, "Lord, do you not care my sister has left me to serve alone? Tell her then to help me." But the Lord answered her, "Martha, Martha, you are anxious and troubled about many things; one thing is needful. Mary has chosen the good portion, which shall not be taken away from her." (Lk. 10:38–42)

Martha's soul is divided. It is given to Jesus but it also to "stuff," and therefore to anxiety—though it was worry that was asphyxiating her spirit, not greed, as it was for Judas. Martha's soul is given to "many things," but Mary's soul is given to Jesus only. Martha is "reasonable," but Mary is not. Mary simply does not worry or calculate about the "many things" when Jesus comes. She won't let any of the many block the Son of the One. She holds nothing back. She does not contracept her love. She gives Him not just her serving, like Martha, but her self. She is the true romantic. She sells all her pearls for one "pearl of great price," risks all her wealth on one investment. She does not use the safety net of a spiritual mutual fund. She knows the holy wildness of all or nothing, of the "one thing needful." She knows that "in the end life contains only one tragedy: not to have been a saint." (Leon Bloy's ending of *The Woman Who Was Poor*) (That one sentence is worth more than all the other books in your library.)

This is true not because sanctity is adorable, but because Christ is. That's what sanctity *means*. There is nothing, literally nothing, in the beauty of the saint except the beauty of Christ. The saint takes an infinite risk, a "leap of faith," and this is beautiful, and also the answer to boredom; but the infinite risk is not the cause of the infinite beauty, the infinite beauty (Christ) is the cause of the infinite risk. If Christ were dead, the leap would *not* be beautiful, good, true, or wonderful. It would be ugly, bad, stupid, and boring. If Jesus is not alive, neither is "Jesus-shock." The effect depends on the cause. If Christ is not raised, our faith is vain and we are pitiable. (I Cor. 15:17–19)

The effect proves the cause. "Jesus-shock" proves that Jesus is alive. Only a live wire can shock you. A dead wire can't.

When the electricity goes out of the wire, everything looks the same. The wire is still there, with the same shape and size and color. Churches still stand, and pews are still occupied. But nobody is shocked.

Are you?

If not, you know Who to go to.

Accept no substitutes. "Little children, keep yourselves from idols."

Part Three:
Jesus-Shock in the Gospels

RATHER THAN *TELLING* YOU, let me *show* you the series of shocks Jesus administers in the Gospels—and continues to administer today, since He is "the same yesterday, today, and forever." (Heb. 13:8) This next section of this book is the most important section of all because it is the data on which all the rest is founded.

Here is an outline of all the passages in the Gospels about "Jesus-shock." I have divided them into categories, moving from the mildest to the strongest kind of shock. Read this section not as something like a school assignment but as a dangerous hunting expedition. The beast you are hunting is alive, and He is "not a tame lion."

A. Shock at Jesus's words, His teachings:
And when Jesus finished these sayings, the crowds were

astonished at his teaching, for he taught them as one who had authority, and not as their scribes. (Matthew 7:28–29)

And on the Sabbath he began to teach in the synagogue; and many who heard him were **astonished**, saying, "Where did this man get all this? What is the wisdom given to him? What mighty works are wrought by his hands! Is this not the carpenter, the son of Mary? (Mark 6:2–4)

After three days they found him in the temple, sitting among the teachers, listening to them and asking them questions; and all who heard him were **amazed** at his understanding and his answers. (Luke 2:46–47)

And all spoke well of him, and **wondered** at the gracious words which proceeded out of his mouth; and they said, "Is this not Joseph's son?" (Luke 4:22)

And they were **astonished** at his teaching, for his word was with authority. (Luke 4:32)

(On the Emmaus Road:) *They said to each other, "Did not our hearts **burn** within us while he talked to us on the road, while he opened to us the Scriptures?"* (Luke 24:32: the Gospel of the Burning Heart)

*"Do not **marvel** that I said to you, 'You must be born anew.' The wind blows where it wills, and you hear the sound of it, but you do not know where it comes from or where it goes; so it is with every one who is born of the Spirit." Nicodemus said to him, "How can this be?"* (John 3:7–9)

The officers then went back to the chief priests and Pharisees, who said to them, "Why did you not bring him?" The officers answered, "No man ever spoke like this man!" (John 7:45–46)

B. Shock at Jesus escaping dilemmas:

And they sent to him some of the Pharisees and some of the Herodians, to entrap him in his talk. And they came and said to him, "Teacher, we know that you are true, and care for no man; for you do not regard the position of men, but truly teach the way of God. It is lawful to pay taxes to Caesar, or not? Should we pay them, or should we not?" But knowing their hypocrisy, he said to them, "Why put me to the test? Bring me a coin, and let me look at it." And they brought one. And he said to them, "Whose likeness and inscription is this?" They said to him, "Caesar's." Jesus said to them, "Render to Caesar the things that are Caesar's, and to

*God the things that are God's." And they were **amazed** at him.* (Mark 12:13–17; cf. Matthew 22:15–22, Luke 20:20–26)

That same day Sadducees came to him, who say that there is no resurrection, and they asked him a question, saying, "Teacher, Moses said, 'If a man dies, having no children, his brother must marry the widow, and raise up children for his brother.' Now there were seven brothers among us; the first married, and died, and having no children left his wife to his brother. So too the second and third, down to the seventh. After them all, the woman died. In the resurrection, therefore, to which of the seven will she be wife? For all had her."

*But Jesus answered them, "You are wrong, because you know neither the Scriptures nor the power of God. For in the resurrection they neither marry nor are given in marriage, but are like angels in heaven. And as for the resurrection of the dead, have you not read what was said to you by God, 'I am the God of Abraham, and the God of Isaac, and the God of Jacob'? He is not God of the dead, but of the living." And when the crowd heard it, they were **astonished** at his teaching.* (Matthew 22: 23–33; cf. Luke 20:27–40)

Now while the Pharisees were gathered together, Jesus

asked them a question, saying, *"What do you think of the Christ? Whose son is he?"* They said to him, *"The son of David."* He said to them, *"How is it then that David, inspired by the Spirit, calls him Lord, saying, 'The Lord said to my Lord, Sit at my right hand till I put your enemies under your feet'? If David thus calls him Lord, how is he his son?"* And no one was able to answer him a word, nor from that day did any one dare to ask him any more questions. (Matthew 22: 41–46; cf. Luke 20:41–44)

After this there was a feast of the Jews, and Jesus went up to Jerusalem. Now there is in Jerusalem by the Sheep Gate a pool, in Hebrew called Bethesda, which has five porticoes. In these lay a multitude of invalids, blind, lame, paralyzed, waiting for the moving of the water; for an angel of the Lord went down at certain seasons into the pool, and troubled the water; whoever stepped in first after the troubling of the water was healed of whatever disease he had. One man was there, who had been ill for 38 years. When Jesus saw him and knew that he had been lying there a long time, he said to him, *"Do you want to be healed?"* The sick man answered him, *"Sir, I have no man to put me into the pool when the water is troubled, and while I am going another steps down before me."* Jesus said to him, *"Rise,*

*take up your pallet and walk." And at once the man
was healed, and he took up his pallet and walked.*
(John 5:1–9)

(This is a dilemma in practice, not theory. In
fact it is a mordantly funny, Monty-Python-like
"Catch-22": the man *needs* to get into the pool
because he is lame, but he *can't* get into the pool—
because he is lame. It's a *koan.*

He is us. We need miraculous healing of our
souls as much as this man needed miraculous healing for his body; but we can't move to get it
because our souls are as lame as his body.

Jesus cuts through the dilemma like Alexander
cutting the Gordian knot. He simply cuts out the
middleman, the angel of healing, and administers
"Jesus-shock" to the lame man. (They are *His*
angels, after all.)

*The scribes and the Pharisees brought a woman who
had been caught in adultery, and placing her in their
midst they said to him, "Teacher, this woman has been
caught in the act of adultery. Now in the law Moses
commanded us to stone such. What do you say about
her?" This they said to test him, that they might have
some charge to bring against him. Jesus bent down and*

*wrote with his finger on the ground. And as they con-
tinued to ask him, he stood up and said to them, "Let
him who is without sin among you be the first to throw
a stone at her." And once more he bent down and wrote
with his finger on the ground. But when they heard it,
they went away, one by one, beginning with the eldest,
and Jesus was left alone with the woman standing
before him. Jesus looked up and said to her, "Woman,
where are they? Has no one condemned you?" She said,
"No one, Lord." And Jesus said, "Neither do I condemn
you; go, and do not sin again."* (John 8:3–11)

Another practical dilemma, and an apparently
unsolvable *koan*. If Jesus answers their question
Yes, tells them to stone the woman, he is as cruel
and legalistic as they are; and he also violates
Roman law, which denied to the Jews the right of
capital punishment even when commanded by
their religious law. If he answers their question No,
and tells them not to stone her, he is a heretic, and
at odds with Moses and therefore with God, who
revealed the Law to Moses. And if He says nothing, or avoids the question, or stalls for time, as He
seems to be doing by writing on the ground, he is
a cowardly cop-out and admits defeat.

Suddenly, like lightening from Heaven, comes

the reply that reveals the presence of something more than human, just as it had happened centuries ago with Solomon, the man with the divine gift of wisdom. (See I Kings 3:28.)

Jesus here reverses the whole relationship, as He always does. They tried to pin him down; He pins them down, revealing Who is the one who is questioning, even when He seems to be the one being questioned, and who are the ones being questioned, even when they seem to be the ones who are asking the questions. The same thing happened to Job. He thought he was testing God, questioning God, seeking God; but all the time God was testing him, questioning him, seeking him. And when He showed up, it was not with answers but with questions.

For He is "I AM," not "He is." He is the First, the Subject, and the Questioner; not the second, the object, and the questioned. "Jesus-shock" comes from the burning bush.

C. Shock at Jesus's healings:

And many were gathered together, so that there was no longer room for them, not even about the door; and he *was preaching the word to them. And they came, bringing to him a paralytic carried by four men. And when they could not get near him because of the crowd, they removed the roof above him; and when they had made an opening, they let down the pallet on which the paralytic lay. And when Jesus saw their faith, he said to the paralytic, "Child, your sins are forgiven." Now some of the scribes were sitting there, questioning in their hearts, "Why does this man speak like this? It is blasphemy! Who can forgive sins but God alone?" And immediately Jesus, perceiving in his spirit that they questioned like this within themselves, said to them, "Why do you question like this in your hearts? Which is easier, to say to the paralytic, 'Your sins are forgiven,' or to say, 'Rise, take up your pallet and walk'? But that you may know that the Son of man has authority on earth to forgive sins"—he said to the paralytic—"I say to you, rise, take up your pallet and go home." And he rose, and immediately took up the pallet and went out before them all; so that they were all **amazed** and glorified God, saying, "We never saw anything like this!"* (Mark 2:2–12; cf. Luke 5: 18–26; Matthew 9:2–8)

And a woman who had a flow of blood for twelve years and had spent all her living upon physicians and could not be healed by any one, came up behind him, and *touched the fringe of his garment; and immediately her flow of blood ceased. And Jesus said, "Who was it that touched me?" When all denied it, Peter said, "Master, the multitudes surround you and press upon you!" But Jesus said, "Some one touched me; for I perceive that power has gone forth from me." And when the woman saw that she was not hidden, she came **trembling**, and falling down before him declared in the presence of all the people why she had touched him, and how she had been immediately healed. And he said to her, "Daughter, your faith has made you well; go in peace."* (Luke 8:43–48; cf. Matthew 9:20–22)

What did the woman receive by touching His garment? Jesus-shock.

*As they were going away, behold, a mute demoniac was brought to him. And when the demon had been cast out, the mute man spoke; and the crowds **marveled**, saying, "Never was anything like this seen in Israel."* (Matthew 9: 32–33)

D. Shock at Jesus's power over nature:

And when he got into the boat, his disciples followed

*him. And behold, there arose a great storm on the sea, so that the boat was being swamped by the waves, but he was asleep. And they went and woke him, saying: "Save us, Lord; we are perishing." And he said to them, "Why are you afraid, O men of little faith?" Then he rose and rebuked the winds and the sea; and there was a great calm. And the men **marveled**, saying, "What sort of man is this, that even winds and sea obey him?"* (Matthew 8:23–27; cf. Luke 8:22–25)

What did He say when He rebuked the winds and the sea? Probably the same thing we say to a dog: "Down, boy!"

Then he made the disciples get into the boat and go before him to the other side, while he dismissed the crowds. And after he had dismissed the crowds, he went up into the hills by himself to pray. When evening came, he was there alone, but the boat by this time was many furlongs distant from the land, beaten by the waves; for the wind was against them. And in the fourth watch of the night he came to them, walking on the sea. But when the disciples saw him walking on the sea, they were terrified, saying, "It is a ghost!" And they cried out for fear. But immediately he spoke to them, saying, "Take heart, it is I; have no fear." And Peter answered him, "Lord, if it is you, bid me come to you on the water." He said, "Come." So Peter got out of the boat and walked on the water and came to Jesus; but when he saw the wind, he was afraid, and beginning to sink he cried out, "Lord, save me." Jesus immediately reached out his hand and caught him, saying to him, "O you of little faith, why did you doubt?" And when they got into the boat, the wind ceased. And those in the boat **worshipped** *him, saying, "Truly you are the Son of God."* (Matthew 14:33)

In the morning, as he was returning to the city, he was hungry. And seeing a fig tree by the wayside he went to it, and found nothing on it but leaves only. And he said to it, "May no fruit ever come from you again!" And the fig tree withered at once. When the disciples saw it they **marveled,** *saying, "How did the fig tree wither at once?"* (Matthew 21:19–20)

. . . he said to Simon, "Put out into the deep and let down your nets for a catch." And Simon answered, "Master, we have toiled all night and took nothing. But at your word I will let down the nets." And when they had done this, they enclosed a great shoal of fish and as their nets were breaking, they beckoned to their partners in the other boat to come and help them. And

*they came and filled both the boats, so that they began
to sink. But when Simon Peter saw it, he fell down at
Jesus' knees saying, "Depart from me, for I am a sinful
man, O Lord." For he was **astonished**, and all that
were with him, at the catch of fish which they were
taken.* (Luke 5:4–9)

E. Shock at Jesus's power over death:

*When they came to the house of the ruler of the syna-
gogue, he saw a tumult, and people weeping and wail-
ing loudly. And when he had entered, he said to them,
"Why do you make a tumult and weep? The child is not
dead but sleeping." And they laughed at him. But he
put them all outside, and took the child's father and
mother and those who were with him and went in
where the child was. Taking her by the hand he said to
her, "Talitha cumi"; which means, "Little girl, I say to
you, arise." And immediately the girl got up and
walked; for she was twelve years old. And immediately they were overcome with **amazement**. And he . . .
told them to give her something to eat."* (Mark
5:38–42; cf. Luke 8:51–56)

(They were too amazed to feed her! Only Jesus
wasn't.)

Soon afterward he went to a city called Nain, and his disciples and a great crowd went with him. As he drew near to the gate of the city, behold, a man who had died was being carried out, the only son of his mother, and she was a widow; and a large crowd from the city was with her. And when the Lord saw her, he had compassion on her and said to her, "Do not weep." And he came and touched the bier, and the bearers stood still. [This is anticipatory Jesus-shock.] *And he said, "Young man, I say to you, arise." And the dead man sat up, and began to speak. And he gave him to his mother. Fear seized them all; and they glorified God, saying, "A great prophet has arisen among us!" and "God has visited his people!"* (Luke 7:11–16)

John 11, the story of the raising of Lazarus, is too long (57 verses) to quote here. Please read it yourself. It is marvelously subtle, multi-layered, nuanced, and detailed. To *see* the Jesus-shock, look at the faces of the disciples when Lazarus comes forth in the scene from the movie *The Greatest Story Ever Told*.

F. Shock at Jesus' own resurrection:

And when the sabbath was past, Mary Magdalene,

*and Mary the mother of James, and Salome, bought spices, to that they might go and anoint him. And very early on the first day of the week they went to the tomb when the sun had risen. And they were saying to one another, "Who will roll away the stone for us from the door of the tomb?" And looking up, they saw that the stone was rolled back; for it was very large. And entering the tomb, they saw a young man sitting on the right side, dressed in a white robe; and they were amazed. And he said to them, "Do not be **amazed**; you seek Jesus of Nazareth, who was crucified. He has risen, he is not here; see the place where they laid him. But go, tell his disciples and Peter that he is going before you to Galilee; there you will see him, as he told you." And they went out and fled from the tomb; for **trembling and astonishment** had come upon them; and they said nothing to any one, for they were **afraid**.* (Mark 16:1–8)*

*But Peter rose and ran to the tomb; stooping and looking in, he saw the linen cloths by themselves; and he went home **wondering** at what had happened.* (Luke 24:12: NB he did not wonder-*what* had happened but wondered-*at* what had happened.)

And as they were saying this, Jesus himself stood

among them, and said to them, "Peace be to you." But they were **startled and frightened**, and supposed that they saw a spirit. And he said to them, "Why are you troubled, and why do questionings rise in your hearts? See my hands and my feet, that it is I myself; handle me, and see; for a spirit has not flesh and bones as you see that I have." And when he had said this he showed them his hands and his feet. And while they still disbelieved for joy, and **wondered**, he said to them, "Have you anything here to eat?" They gave him a piece of broiled fish, and he took it and ate it before them. (Luke 24:36–43)

G. Shock at Jesus's power over demons:

Then a blind and deaf demoniac was brought to him, and he healed him, so that the mute man spoke and saw. And all the people were **amazed**, and said, "Can this be the son of David?" (Matthew 12:22–23)

And immediately there was in their synagogue a man with an unclean spirit; and he cried out, "What have you to do with us, Jesus of Nazareth? Have you come to destroy us? I know who you are, the Holy One of God." But Jesus rebuked him, saying, "Be silent and

*come out of him!" And the unclean spirit, convulsing
him and crying with a loud voice, came out of him.
And they were all **amazed**, so that they questioned
among themselves, saying, "What is this? A new teaching! With authority he commands even the unclean
spirits, and they obey him." And at once his fame
spread everywhere throughout all the surrounding
region of Galilee.* (Mark 1:23–28; cf. Luke 4:33–37)

After Jesus exorcised the Gadarene demoniac
(whose name was "Legion": Luke 8:30), *Then all
the people of the surrounding country of the Gadarenes
asked him to depart from them; for they were **seized
with great fear**."* (Luke 8:37; cf. Matthew 8:34)

H. Shock at Jesus turning to hostility:

The above incident among the Gadarenes is one
example of this. Others are:

*And the chief priests and the scribes . . . sought a way
to destroy him; for they **feared** him, because all the multitude was **astonished** at his teaching.* (Mark 11:18)

After Jesus healed a man's withered hand on the
Sabbath, *they were **filled with fury** and discussed*

with one another what the might do to Jesus. (Luke 6:11)

I. Shock at our own lack of faith:

*And he **marveled** because of their unbelief.* (Mark 6:6)

"You search the scriptures, because you think that in them you have eternal life; and it is they that bear witness to me; yet you refuse to come to me that you may have life." (John 5:39–40)

What irony! Imagine Juliet knocking on Romeo's door, and Romeo refusing to open to her because he had his nose in a book: his scrapbook of her photographs!

J. Shock at His divinity:

And he was transfigured before them, and his face shone like the sun, and his garments became white as light . . . a bright cloud overshadowed them, and a voice from the cloud said, "This is my beloved Son, *with whom I am well pleased; listen to him." When the disciples heard this, they fell on their faces, and were filled with **awe**.* (Matthew 17:2, 5, 6)

*And when Elizabeth heard the greeting of Mary, the child leaped in her womb; and Elizabeth was filled with the Holy Spirit and she **exclaimed** with a loud cry, "Blessed are you among women, and blessed is the fruit of your womb!"* (Luke 1:41–42: the poet wrote that when Jesus turned water into wine at Cana, the water saw the face of its God and blushed; here, the baby prophet saw his God and jumped.)

"Because I said to you, I saw you under the fig tree, do you believe? You shall see greater things than these." And he said to him, "Truly, truly, I say to you, you will see heaven opened, and the angels of God ascending and descending upon the Son of man." (John 1:50–51)

*Pilate said unto them, "Take him yourselves and crucify him, for I find no crime in him." The Jews answered him, "We have a law, and by that law he ought to die; because he has made himself the Son of God." When Pilate heard these words, he was even more **afraid**; he* *entered the praetorium again and said to Jesus, "Where are you from?"* (John 19: 6–9)

There are two kinds of "Jesus-shock." To the evil and dishonest it brings terror; to the good, it brings wonder and joy. Contrast with Pilate the following:

But Mary stood weeping outside the tomb, and as she wept she stooped to look into the tomb; and she saw two angels in white, sitting where the body of Jesus had lain, one at the head and one at the feet. They said to her, "Woman, why are you weeping?" She said to them, "Because they have taken away my Lord, and I do not know where they have laid him." Saying this, she turned round and saw Jesus standing, but she did not know that it was Jesus. Jesus said to her, "Woman, why are you weeping? Whom do you seek?" Supposing him to be the gardener, she said to him, "Sir, if you have carried him away, tell me where you have laid him, and I will take him away." Jesus said to her, "Mary." She turned and said to him in Hebrew, "Rabboni!" (which means Teacher). (John 20:11–16)

Then he said to Thomas, "Put your finger here, and see my hands, and put out your hand, and place it in my side; do not be faithless, but believing." Thomas answered him, "My Lord and my God!" (John 20:27–28)

K. Other shocks at seeing Him:

And immediately all the crowd, when they saw him, were greatly **amazed**. (Mark 9:15)

And the chief priests accused him of many things. And Pilate again asked him, "Have you no answer to make? See how many charges they bring against you." But Jesus made no further answer, so that Pilate **wondered**. (Mark 15:3–5)

Now his parents went to Jerusalem every year at the feast of the Passover. And when he was twelve years old, they went up according to custom; and when the feast was ended, as they were returning, the boy Jesus stayed behind in Jerusalem. His parents did not know it, but supposing him to be in the company they went a day's journey, and they sought him among their kinsfolk and acquaintances; and when they did not find him, they returned to Jerusalem, seeking him. After three days they found him in the temple, sitting among *the teachers, listening to them and asking them questions; and all who heard him were **amazed** at his understanding and his answers. And when they saw him they were **astonished***. (Luke 2:41–48)

L. Shock at His "I AM" claims:

The depth of the shock administered here cannot be understood without understanding that no Jew would ever dream of uttering the self-revealed Name of God Himself, the sacred Tetragrammaton (four-letter-word) JHWH ("I AM") which God had revealed to Moses in the Burning Bush as His own eternal name, and which no human being dared to utter because unlike all other words, "I AM" cannot be uttered in the second or third person ("you are" or "he is") but only in the first. In other words, to utter this word is to claim to be God, in as explicit, as uncompromising, and as confrontational a way as was humanly possible. It was the absolute apotheosis of blasphemy—unless it was God Himself uttering it.

In at least one of the following utterances (John 8:58), Jesus clearly uses this word, for there is no predicate after it. In the other cases, the situation, the reaction, and the shock suggests that He did.

In some cases, the shock happens when the shadowy figure of the "Messiah" ("the (God-) Anointed One"—the literal meaning of "Christ") leaps to life out of the pages of prophecy (John 4; John 5:39–40), as does the figure from Daniel's prophecy, the "Son of man" (John 9:35–38). In other cases, the shock happens when something abstract (e.g. "way," "truth," "life") suddenly becomes concrete, something impersonal (e.g. "bread," "door") becomes personal, or something a person *has* becomes something He *is*. For God does not *have*, or share, or receive, or participate in, any attributes: He *is* all His attributes. He does not *have* goodness or truth or beauty; He *is* goodness, and truth, and beauty. He does not even *have* being; He *is* being. Note all the "I ams" in the following:

The woman said to him, "I know that Messiah is com-
ing (he who is called Christ); when he comes he will
show us all things." Jesus said to her, "I who speak to
you am he." (John 4:25–26: the tipping point in the long, delicate scene of Jesus and the woman at the well. Read the whole chapter (4) in this light.)

*Jesus said to them, "Truly, truly I say to you, it was not Moses who gave you the bread from heaven; my Father gives you the true bread from heaven. For the bread of God is that which comes down from heaven and gives life to the world." They said to him, "Lord, give us this bread always." Jesus said to them, "**I am** the bread of life; he who comes to me shall not hunger, and he who believes in me shall never thirst."*

*"**I am** the bread of life. Your fathers ate the manna in the wilderness, and they died. This is the bread which comes down from heaven, that a man may eat of it and not die. **I am** the living bread which came down from heaven; if any one eats of this bread, he will live for ever; and the bread which I shall give for the life of the world is my flesh."*

The Jews then disputed among themselves, saying, "How can this man give us his flesh to eat?" So Jesus said to them, "Truly, truly, I say to you, unless you eat the flesh of the Son of man and drink his blood, you have no life in you; he who eats my flesh and drinks my blood has eternal life, and I will raise him up at the last day. For my flesh is food indeed, and my blood is drink indeed. He who eats my flesh and drinks my blood abides in me, and I in him. As the living Father sent me, and I live because of the Father, so he who eats me will live because of me." (John 6:32–35; 48–57)

Jesus spoke to them, saying, "*I am the light of the world; he who follows me will not walk in darkness, but will have the light of life.*" (John 8:12)

"*You will die in your sins unless you believe that **I am he**.*" They said to him, "*Who are you?*" Jesus said to them, "*Even what I have told you from the beginning.*" (John 8:24–25)

So Judas, procuring a band of soldiers and some officers from the chief priests and the Pharisees, went there with lanterns and torches and weapons. Then Jesus, knowing all that was to befall him, came forward and said to them, "*Whom do you seek?*" They answered him, "*Jesus of Nazareth.*" Jesus said to them, "*I am he.*" Judas, who betrayed him, was standing with them. When he said to them, "*I am he,*" they draw back and fell to the ground." (John 18:3–6)

"*Your father Abraham rejoiced to see my day; he saw it and was glad.*" The Jews then said to him, "*You are not yet fifty years old, and have you seen Abraham?*" Jesus said to them, "*Truly, truly, I say to you, before Abraham was, **I AM**.*" So they took up stones to throw at him. (John 8:56–59)

"I and the Father are one." The Jews took up stones again to stone him. (John 10:30–31)

*Jesus . . . said, "Do you believe in the Son of man?" He answered, "And who is he, sir, that I may believe in him?" Jesus said to him, "You have seen him, and **it is he** who speaks to you." He said, "Lord, I believe"; and he worshipped him.* (John 9:35–38)

*So Jesus again said to them, "Truly, truly, I say to you, **I am** the door of the sheep . . . **I am** the door; if any one enters by me, he will be saved, and will go in and out and find pasture. . . . **I am** the good shepherd."* (John 10:7, 9, 14: cf. Ezekiel 34 on this Messianic prophecy.)

*"**I am** the Son of God"* (John 10:36)

*Jesus said to her, "Your brother will rise again." Martha said to him, "I know that he will rise again in the resurrection at the last day." Jesus said to her, "**I am** the resurrection and the life; he who believes in me, though he die, yet shall he live, and whoever lives and believes in me shall never die. Do you believe this?" She said to him, "Yes, Lord; I believe that you are the*

Christ, the Son of God, he who is coming into the world." (John 11:23–27)

Notice carefully: He does not merely *cause* the resurrection; He *is* the resurrection. Before He calls forth Lazarus's body from the dead past of the tomb into the present, He calls forth Martha's faith from the future "resurrection at the last day" into the present.

Thomas said to him, "Lord, we do not know where you are going; how can we know the way?" Jesus said to him, "I am the way, and the truth, and the life; no one comes to the Father, but by me." (John 14:6)

Again: he does not *point* the way, *teach* the truth, and *bring* the life; He *is* the way, the truth, and the life. Pilate's skeptical sneer "What is truth?" was addressed to Truth Himself, standing there right in front of his face. The world's stupidest question was three words; God's profoundest answer was one Word.

Part Four: The Foundation: Real Presence

WE HAVE SEEN THE shattering, revolutionary effect of "Jesus-shock" in the New Testament. Now let us see its cause.

Its cause is obviously nothing less than Jesus Himself, not any technique He uses, any "charismatic" quality of personality He manifests, or the content of the words He uses; for techniques, qualities of personality, or content of words can be reduplicated by others, while no one and nothing can ever reduplicate Jesus. No one ever has and no one ever will. Nothing less than Jesus can be the cause of "Jesus-shock."

Anyone can be a Buddha. Buddha himself repeatedly said this: "Be lamps unto yourselves." In other words, "You are the light of the world." But Jesus said, "I am the light of the world." For only Jesus can be Jesus.

Buddha said: "Look not to me, look to my *dharma* [doctrine]." Jesus said: "Come unto Me."

And it is not just the *existence* of Jesus, for that has always been there: Jesus has always existed. He is eternal. And not just the *power* of Jesus or the *love* of Jesus or the *wisdom* of Jesus, for they have been there as long as Jesus has been there: from the beginning. No, it is only the *real presence* of Jesus that produces "Jesus-shock."

What is "presence"? "Presence" is a very easy thing to know (*kennen, connaitre*) and a very hard thing to understand (*wissen, savoir*). It is easy to detect. Uneducated people, small children, severely retarded people, even animals, often detect it better than educated, brilliant people do, for the simple have no hiding places. Yet, though it is very easy to be aware of, it is very hard to define—perhaps impossible.

Let's try anyway. Since human persons are neither pure spirits nor pure animals, but both together, let's see whether the presence of these persons is spiritual or physical or both.

If I accidentally bump into you and knock you down in the street but do not recognize you and merely utter a sincere "Oh, I'm sorry" without seeing your face, that is not real presence. So real presence—the real presence of a person—is not just physical presence.

On the other hand, if I am thinking about you personally, even loving you, with both my will and my emotions, but you are thousands of miles away from me, that is not real presence either. You are *absent*, though "absence makes the heart grow fonder"—sometimes. So real presence is not just mental presence, presence to mind and will and emotions.

And it is not even just the combination of the two. For if I believe you are a thousand miles away, and I am thinking of you and loving you, and I happen to bump into you in the street and knock you down and say I'm sorry, but do not know that it is you, that is not real presence either, even though it is both physical presence and mental presence. Real presence includes both physical and mental presence, but it is also something more.

It is hard to define that "something more" because it is not an essence but an existence. "*What* is presence?" cannot be answered because it is not a "what" at all but the "thereness" or "hereness" of a "what." It can be shown but not defined. It can be pointed to but not circumscribed. It is like a fire.

Remember Job's three friends, who talked

about God, with theological correctness, as if He were absent, while Job talked *to* Him, as present, though his ideas about Him were confused and mistaken. Job was rewarded: God appeared to Job, but not to the three friends (42:5). And He said that the three had not "spoken rightly" of Him, but Job had (42:7). Why? Because Job had practiced God's presence: he prayed. He alone talked *to* God as present even though he did not *feel* that presence. The three "friends" were deists. Most theists are deists most of the time, in practice if not in theory. They practice the absence of God instead of the presence of God.

We have seen, in our thought experiment above, that the real presence of a person to another person is more than just objective and physical, and more than just subjective and mental or psychological, and more than both together. Perhaps it is impossible to define (for what else is there besides the objective and the subjective?), but you can't miss it.

Now this personal presence of Christ is well known by Protestant Evangelicals (though not *only* by them, of course). It is their "specialty," so to speak, and God bless them for it! They "accept the Lord Jesus Christ as their personal Lord and

Savior." (They say they are suspicious of liturgical formulas, but they are not; they are human.) In this favorite formula of theirs, "personal" does not mean "subjective" or "merely individual," like my personal preference for black raspberry ice cream, but "personally present as a divine Person to this human person who acknowledges Him and believes in Him."

But where is this presence most completely available? Where does the Christ believed in, trusted, and adored by Evangelicals make Himself most completely present, in His "body and blood, soul and divinity"? Is He *always equally and completely* present to the Evangelical in prayer? In Bible reading? In acts of charity done in His name? No. Though He is indeed really present there, that presence varies because it is partly dependent on the soul of the believer. It is indeed the same Jesus who was present in the streets of Jerusalem and on the Cross, who is present to the Evangelical believer, but not in the same way, not as really, totally, objectively, ontologically, or completely present. In Catholic theological terms, prayer and scripture and Christian service are sacramentals, but not sacraments.

There is only one place where He is always

completely present, and every Christian in the world knew it until the Protestant Reformation: in the Eucharist.

Christians worship Christ because Christ is God. Catholics worship the Eucharist because the Eucharist is Christ. Under the appearances of bread and wine, He is literally just as fully and truly and really and objectively and ontologically present to the Catholic who adores Him there and who receives Him there in Holy Communion, as He was to His disciples in Palestine for three years. In fact, more so, until the Last Supper, when they too were privileged to eat His body and drink His blood and get Him inside themselves instead of just outside.

This is perhaps the single most controversial of all Catholic doctrines. It generated the most controversy and passion and ire and war at the time of the Reformation. Read the history of the wars of the Reformation in primary sources and you will discover this.

Once you think about it, it is an "of course." For if Protestants are right, Catholics are the most ridiculous heretics and idolaters imaginable, worshipping bread and wine. That's as bad as the pagan worshipping sacred sticks or stones. We all know God's judgment on *that*: just read the Old Testament. It violates the very first and greatest commandment of all, the commandment against idolatry, which is worshipping the wrong God, worshipping a creature rather than the Creator. This is no technical, esoteric, arcane, specialized, out-in-left-field theological mistake; this is just about the spiritually stupidest mistake we can possibly make. And Catholics make it, every Sunday, at every Mass, if Protestants are right. Compared with this, disputes between Protestants and Catholics about Church authority, or Mary, or the saints, or Purgatory, or Bible interpretation, or baptism, or predestination, are almost trivial.

On the other hand, if Catholics are right, then Protestants are missing out on the most perfect, intimate, and complete union with their Lord that is possible in this life. As in the famous painting, Christ is knocking at their door, and they are not opening it because they deny it is really He. They are like 1st-century Jews who rejected their God when He appeared to them in the flesh because they refused to believe that God would come in disguise; they did not have the faith to see the invisible God in the visible human appearances. They were hung up on the physical appearances. It is they, not Catholics, who are the idolaters of the physical, the creaturely.

This issue seems non-negotiable. Other issues are more negotiable. Justification by Faith has already been negotiated. The doctrine of *sola fides*, which all Evangelicals regard as the essence and *sine qua non* of Protestantism, the doctrine that Luther thought justified breaking with Rome because it concerned the infinitely important question "What must I do to be saved?"—this issue has been solved and overcome! The news has not yet leaked through to the average Christian, Protestant or Catholic, but if you look at the Joint Statement on Justification, approved by the Vatican and many official Protestant authorities, especially Lutherans, you will find that this miracle has indeed taken place. After hundreds of years of condemning each other's souls to hell and bodies to battlefield graves, Protestants and Catholics have concluded that they were both saying essentially the same thing in different words, and fighting about the words rather than the real thing. (That is of course an oversimplification, but it is not a falsehood.)

And the issue of "*sola gratia*" was solved long ago by the Council of Trent, which affirmed the total primacy and priority of grace as strongly as the Reformers did. They simply added the point that grace turned us and our free will and our good works on, not off.

And the third "*sola*," "*sola scriptura*," may some day be solved as well, though it has not yet reached that point, and it seems beyond anyone's ability yet to see how it is possible for both sides to agree without compromise on this issue. But it seemed equally impossible half a century ago for anyone to see how both sides could ever agree without compromise on Justification by Faith (except Von Balthasar, as early as the '50's, in his doctoral dissertation on Luther and justification). If *that* sticking point was resolved, this one may be resolved too some day.

So all three non-negotiable "*solas*" of the Reformation may be resolvable. But the Real Presence remains the stone of stumbling.

Look at history. (This is the single clearest reason why I became a Catholic: because I looked at history.) Not a single Christian in the world for 1000 years doubted or denied the Real Presence of Christ in the Eucharist. The 11th-century heretic Berengar of Tours was the first, and there were no others until the 16th century, except the heretical

Waldensians and Albigensians. The Albigensians were the most hated and feared heretics in the history of Christendom, and they were totally wiped out either by plague, persecution, birth dearth, or repentance. The center of all Christian worship until the Reformation was always the Eucharist, not the sermon, as it is for Protestants. The Eucharist was never omitted, as it usually is for Protestants. Any pre-Reformation Christian would see a church service without the Eucharist as something like a marriage without sex.

Now comes the supreme irony. What is it that the Eucharist provides? The very thing Protestant Evangelicals cherish the most: the Real Presence of Christ and our real union with Christ, "accepting the Lord Jesus Christ as your personal Savior" in the most real, total, complete, personal, concrete, and intimate way!

The connection between the "Protestant point" (Christ as personal Lord and Savior) and the "Catholic point" (the Real Presence of Christ in the Eucharist) is closer than a bridge; it is virtually an identity. This has to be a central key to ecumenism and reunion. Put the Protestant flint and the Catholic steel together, and you will kindle a fire that will burn round the world.

Are you a Protestant who wants to do full justice to accepting Christ as your Lord? Then learn to adore Him in the Eucharist, as Catholics do, for He is there. Are you a Catholic who wants to do full justice to His presence in the Eucharist? Then learn to love and trust Him as your personal Lord and Savior as Evangelicals do, for He is that.

The Eucharist is not a contrast to the "Protestant point." It is not even an addition to the "Protestant point." It *is* the "Protestant point." It is the Lord Jesus Christ, the Savior, your Savior, *acting as* your Savior, saving you by giving you Himself, His whole self, body and blood, soul and divinity. (If any part of that were omitted, you could not be saved.) The Eucharist is how He has willed to get salvation—gets Himself—*into* you.

There is a similar identity between the Real Presence and the "Jesus-shock" that we saw in the Gospels. We too can experience the same "Jesus-shock," the same revolutionary effects, that people experienced in Palestine 2000 years ago. Although the mental and emotional elements of that first surprise are not possible any longer because we already know Him, yet the deeper, long-range, revolutionary, life-transforming effects are equally present today because He is equally present today.

He may not be *new* to us as He was to His apostles, but He is the same ("Jesus Christ, the same yesterday, today, and forever."—Heb. 13:8), and therefore He *is* new to us too. He is "that Beauty ancient yet ever new."

And He is here! He did not just rise, He *is* risen. The total ontological identity between the Christ of the 1st century and the Christ of the 21st century trumps the mental and emotional difference between the surprise of the first and the familiarity of the 21st.

And even the mental and emotional shock returns every time we pay attention. (Attention is very rare and very precious. In Heaven we will be all attention.) If we continue to remember Who this is, and what He is doing, and why He is doing it, it will continue to be shocking, as it was when we watched *The Passion of the Christ.*

Protestants want to become saints just as much as Catholics do. And this is one of the many very good reasons to become Catholics. For two of the most perfect and powerful means to becoming a saint are Eucharistic adoration and frequent Holy Communion—not because they are liturgically correct, and not because they are psychologically useful, but because Jesus Christ the saint-maker is present in the Eucharist as He is nowhere else in the world. And wherever He is present, He is active. Even when He waits patiently in the Tabernacle, disguised behind the appearances of a little wafer of bread, He is acting. ("Waiting" is an action too.)

* * * * *

As a young Protestant at Calvin College, I read the early Church Fathers to try to prove to myself that I was in the right church, that Christ had established a "Protestant" style church that gradually went Catholic, and that the Protestant reformers didn't depart from the religion of the Apostles and start a new church but rather restored the old one by purging it of medieval, unbiblical, pagan, heretical accretions, like a sailor scraping barnacles off his ship. So I focused on what Catholics believed and Protestants didn't, especially the Papacy, devotion and prayers to saints, reverence to Mary, Purgatory, the priesthood, the Mass, and the Eucharist. (These last three are three aspects of the same mystery.)

I found that all of these doctrines were there very early, but some of them developed gradually, for instance Marian devotion and theology, and also the degree of the explicitness of the universality of the authority of the Bishop of Rome. (I need all four "ofs" to say this correctly.) Although I often found silence on these "Catholic" points in the Fathers of the Church, I never found protests or protestants. I never found a single one of the current Protestant objections to a single one of the current Catholic doctrines in a single one of the early Christian writers. For the first 1000 years, no one ever protested against any of the specifically Catholic doctrines which Protestants claimed were innovations. Was the Holy Spirit asleep for a millennium?

And I found that three doctrines that were as essential to Protestants as they were to Catholics, namely the Trinity, the Incarnation (that is, the two natures of Christ), and the canon of the New Testament, "developed" (that is, our understanding of them developed; they were "unpacked") just as gradually as these other, specifically Catholic doctrines did. They came like tides rather than like storms.

But as a Protestant I was the most shocked by the centrality of the Eucharist for Christian worship from the earliest times, and by the universal, unquestioned belief in the Real Presence. Even

Luther did not deny the Real Presence. Nor do Lutherans today. Nor do Anglicans. Even Calvin believed it was an objectively efficacious "sign *and seal*," not a mere symbol. Until Zwingli, no orthodox, traditional, nonheretical, mainline, historic, apostolic Christian ever believed what most Protestants believe today about the Eucharist: that it is only a holy symbol of Christ, not Christ Himself.

This doctrine was assured by the old formula of Vincent of Lerins: "what has been believed by all, at all times, in all places." It was also assured by the rules of logical consistency. For the very same teaching authority that assured me of the Trinity and the Incarnation and the canon of scripture, assured me of the Real Presence. All these doctrines all stood on exactly the same foundation. And the name of that foundation, the name of that teaching authority, is the "one holy, Catholic, and apostolic Church," which was also believed by all Christians for 1500 years. Not *a* church but *the* Church. Christ is not a polygamist.

Protestants will point out that I had learned all these fundamental Christian doctrines from scripture. Yes, but only as taught and interpreted by the Church, which as a matter of historical fact had always been the standard for Christian orthodoxy in interpreting scripture. Scripture itself calls the Church "the pillar and ground of the truth." (I Tim. 3:15) Scripture was the Church's textbook, but the Church was the living teacher who taught and interpreted that textbook.

Scripture does not always interpret itself. All heretics appealed to scripture too. Deniers of the Trinity and the Incarnation also appealed to scripture. The words "Trinity" and "Incarnation" do not appear anywhere in scripture, any more than the words "Eucharist" or "Purgatory" or "papacy" do. And the canon of scripture is not in scripture! No one of these doctrines is so clear in scripture that it cannot be denied. In fact, all of them *were* denied by heretics. It was in fact the Church that defined doctrine, crafted creeds, and authoritatively anathematized.

If you deny the infallibility of the Church, you will inevitably deny the infallibility of scripture sooner or later, as the history of Protestantism shows. For no effect can be greater than its cause. Why trust the Teacher's Book if you do not trust the Teacher?

Thus Modernism always sets in, given enough time. Even Southern Baptists will be Modernists in another century or two. There are many Catholic Modernists too, but they are officially condemned by the Church. The Catholic Church is the only church that never succumbed to any heresy in all her history. No other church has verified Christ's promise to "guide into all truth" (Jn. 16:13) and to teach with His own authority ("He who hears you, hears Me")—an authority which is infallible, unless Christ Himself is fallible and thus not divine. Throughout history, the Church's *magisterium* (teaching authority) has always been like a sea wall against which the waves of heresy crash repeatedly, and end up recoiling upon themselves, leaving the inhabited houses along the shoreline safe and dry. The frowning, formidable face that Holy Mother Church turns to heretics is only for the sake of the smiling face she turns to her own children. Mother Bear protects her cubs.

* * * * *

Protestants usually believe (1) that there are only two sacraments, not seven; and, more importantly (because quality is more important than quantity), (2) that the sacraments do not give grace objectively, by themselves, (*"ex opera operato"*), as God Himself does, but subjectively, by the individual's own faith and piety. Protestants believe that the sacraments are like ladders that God gave to us by which we can climb up to Him. Catholics believe that they are like ladders that God gave to Himself by which He climbs down to us. The Catholic view of the sacraments is that they are the means of salvation; that God really forgives your sins when the priest pronounces absolution in Christ's name and in His authority; that God really regenerates your soul and removes Original Sin when you are baptized; that Christ really unites Himself to your soul in a spiritual marriage when you receive Holy Communion. Catholics believe that the sacraments are the answer to Kierkegaard's question (in his *Philosophical Fragments* and *Concluding Unscientific Postscript*) of how we cross over 2000 years and become "contemporary with Christ," or rather how Christ crosses over and becomes contemporary with us. The answer is that we meet not just spiritually and subjectively, in our minds; we meet materially and objectively in and through the matter of the sacraments. Matter matters!

When as a Protestant I discovered that this was what the Catholic Church taught about sacraments, I was shocked. It seemed crude, materialistic, externalistic. And it seemed "magical":

automatic and impersonal. That objection, I found, was easily disposed of: it is a sheer misunderstanding. The sacraments are *not* "magical" because they are not automatic. We can block the grace, and we usually do, more or less, like stopping down a faucet, or pulling down the window blinds. But the water, or the light, comes from God, not from us. Christ really comes to meet us and sanctify us in the sacraments, however little we may appreciate Him.

Magic is a one-way operation, like nailing wood. The wood is passive. But sacraments are two-way operations, like sexual intercourse. He is a gentleman; he seduces but He does not rape. We are not rendered passive by His grace, but active. Sacramental grace, like all grace, works like a two-part epoxy glue, to glue together our souls and our Savior. The analogy of the epoxy is imperfect because half of the binding power comes from each half of an epoxy, but all the power in the sacraments comes from God. But the analogy does make one valid point: that both parts, ours and God's, are necessary. It's not just God, doing automatic magic without our free will. We can't get grace without God's free will to give it, but God won't give grace without our free will to accept it, to trust it, to believe in it. (The Bible identifies "believing" with "receiving": cf. Jn 1:12). God can supply grace without sacraments, but He cannot supply our faith without our consent. That is why God's sacraments without our faith do not save us (they are not magic), but our faith without His sacraments can save us, for God can make up for His missing half of the epoxy (the sacraments) but He cannot make up for our missing half (our faith).

So when a Protestant is saved by faith alone without the sacraments, *that* is the miracle, that is the unusual thing, the thing outside the divinely appointed order of things; that is getting into God's house through the back door. But when a Catholic is saved by faith *and* the sacraments, that is the usual thing, that is the front door, that is the full epoxy.

Sacraments are like hoses. They are the channels of the living water of God's grace. Our faith is like opening the faucet. We can open it a lot, a little, or not at all. When the faucet handle is turned off, no water flows to us, even though the water is still objectively present. When it is "turned on" by faith, the water flows out and into us, and we get wet. But the water is already there. The faucet itself does not bring the water, only stop it down. We can block it, but we cannot produce it. But God can get the water to us even without using the hose.

Protestantism is still Christianity, but not complete Christianity, because it denies "*ex opere operato*" sacraments. ("*Ex opere operato*" means "by the work of the (divine) working" rather than "by the work of the (human) one worked on," or "*ex opere operantis*".) Shocking and offensive as this sounds to Protestants, Protestant "churches" are not really churches, because there is only one Church, and it has apostolic succession and a priesthood that is authorized to bring about Christ's Real Presence in the sacraments. (The priest only catalyzes the reaction, so to speak; God causes it. The priest does not create; he procreates.) Protestant "churches" do not have apostolic succession in any one of the three divinely appointed Old Testament offices of prophet, priest, or king. They do not have apostolic succession of consecrated bishops, who are the locus of the Church's prophetic teaching authority. They do not have apostolic succession of consecrated priests who are the agents of Christ's Real Presence in the sacraments. And they do not have the apostolic succession of authority to rule in Christ's name. That is why the Church politely calls them "ecclesial communities" but not "churches."

But Protestantism is still Christianity. It lacks the fullness of the Church and the sacraments, but as the Church herself says in her official *Catechism*, "God can also work outside His sacraments." And He often does. Protestantism is still the Gospel. It can save you. For it introduces you to the Savior. Hinduism, or Buddhism, or Islam cannot save you, though many things in them can make you very wise and good. Only Christ can save you. When Hindus or Buddhists or Muslims are saved, they are not saved by their religion but by Christ, anonymously.

So the sacraments are not "magic." But as a Protestant I found in myself another objection to sacramentalism that was even more fundamental: that it was "pagan," i.e. *materialistic*. According to the Catholic Church, if you received the Catholic Eucharist, consecrated by a Catholic or Orthodox priest who had been validly ordained by the chain of apostolic succession stretching back to the Apostles, who were ordained by Christ, then you really received Christ; but if you received the Eucharist from a Protestant clergyperson, however holy he or she may have been, and however holy you yourself may have been, and however deep and passionate your faith and hope and love may have been at the moment you ate the holy bread and drank the holy wine, you were *not* receiving the literal, objectively real body and blood, soul and divinity of Christ Himself. You were only having a religious experience.

This shocked me. Then, gradually, I became shocked at my shock. For I realized that I was a Gnostic. I found that many other things I believed, or thought I believed, as a Protestant because they were in the Bible, were equally shocking and "materialistic." For instance, if that woman with the lifelong hemorrhage in Luke 8:43–48: had touched the hem of St. Peter's garment, or anyone else's, sincerely believing it was the hem of Christ's garment, she would *not* have received the miracle of healing that He felt "go out from" Him. If St. John had mistakenly stood under the wrong cross and the blood of the Good Thief had dripped onto his head, he would not have received the divine Precious Blood of salvation, even if his soul had been in a holy state. If Christ had not literally, physically died, had not literally shed His blood, but only come to preach and teach and heal, we could not be saved. God is incredibly materialistic! And the Sacraments, as understood by Catholics, were merely the logical extension of the Incarnation. Same divine policy. Not "have the wrong thoughts and you fall" but "eat this forbidden fruit and you fall." Not "have good intentions and you are saved" but "receive the body and blood of the Savior and you are saved." (I Cor. 11:27–29)

So I gradually came to realize that the Catholic doctrine of the Sacraments was not an addition to the "mere Christianity" of the apostles and the New Testament, but that the Protestant doctrine was a subtraction from it.

This was a shock. Of course it was, for I was not just dealing with a doctrine here, I was dealing with a Tiger. (William Blake called Him "Christ the Tiger." C.S. Lewis called Him a lion.)

There is a danger among "cradle Catholics" that familiarity dulls this shock, builds up immunity to it. This is not inevitable. The saints do not build up immunity to the shock. As they become ever more familiar with Christ, "Jesus-shock" increases rather than decreases.

There is also a danger among Catholic "intellectuals" that the doctrine of the Real Presence becomes a substitute for the Real Presence; that it is looked-at rather than looked-along, like the famous finger pointing at the moon, or like Job's three friends treating their theology of God as if it were God. Job's theology was wrong, but it was transparent. He dealt with God, not just with ideas. He looked-along his ideas, however confused and wrong they were, and looked-at God, however blinkingly and blindedly, while the three friends looked at their correct ideas instead of looking-along them; thus they never saw God, while Job did. (see Job 42:1–6)

C.S. Lewis explains this important philosophical point, the distinction between looking-at and looking-along, in his essay "Meditation in a Toolshed." *Everything* in this world is to be looked-along, and God looked-at, for everything is a means and God is the end. Everything is only a creature and becomes an idol when treated as the Creator. Everything is relative and God alone is the Absolute. Christ is both absolute and relative, both God and Man, both Creator and creature, both God, to look at, and an icon of God, to look along; both God Himself and the Word *of* God.

Eventually I realized that I, like most Protestants, had been infected with Gnosticism ("spirituality—a dreadful doom," says Chesterton).

And I realized that there are two kinds of Gnosticism: intellectual Gnosticism and emotional Gnosticism, and that I had been guilty of both, but especially emotional Gnosticism. I had substituted pious feelings about Christ for the Real Presence of Christ. I had been very impressed by a serious skeptic's argument against the Real Presence. He said something like this: "All these holy communions, thousands of them over a lifetime, and each one as real as if Christ Himself appeared in our streets—and what difference does it make? I can't see the difference. I can't feel the difference. If that's really Jesus, how can He not make a tremendous difference? Why aren't all Catholics tremendously holier and happier than everybody else, if they've got the Real Presence of Jesus Christ?" That was almost the same question I had Socrates ask his fellow students at Harvard Divinity School. (See page 39.)

We did see Him in ancient Israel, and we do sometimes feel Him in our hearts, and those are two precious presences; but we do *not* see Him in the Eucharist, and we usually do *not* feel His presence there. It is sheer faith, not sense or feeling, which accepts Him there. And that is much more precious than sight or feeling. We are more privileged than Christ's Apostles. He says that Himself to us when he says to Doubting Thomas, "You have believed because you have seen me. Blessed are those who have not seen, and yet believe." (Jn. 20:29)

Do we believe that? It doesn't *feel* more blessed to believe without seeing. If we saw Him now, in a vision, or if we could get into a time machine and see Him in 30 A.D. in Israel, it would certainly *feel* more blessed. We would feel on top of the world. But He tells us that this appearance deceives us. It is like telling us that the sky is not blue. How can we believe such a thing? Because it is He who tells us. After all, we believe our scientists when they tell us that solid matter is not solid, that space is curved and time is relative—and that the sky is not, in fact, blue at all, it only appears blue because it absorbs other colors and reflects blue away. Why are we more willing to believe our scientists when they speak of the creation than we are to believe the Creator when He speaks of Himself?

What is precious in believing-without-seeing is not the not-seeing but the believing, the strengthening of the faith muscle when the crutches of seeing and feeling are removed. Seeing Him was not enough, for thousands saw Him yet turned away, and even shouted, "Crucify him!" Feeling Him in the heart is not enough either, for that is subjective, that is ours, that is fallible. Furthermore, we are all self-centered experience-addicts. We are so addicted to our own positive experiences of joy and happiness that if we experienced Christ more joyfully than we do, we would almost inevitably come to love our experience of Christ more than Christ Himself. We would come to worship our own experience, that is, ourselves. We can be quite sure that He knows exactly what He is doing in keeping us in "the dark night of the soul" emotionally as well as intellectually, in training us to rely on faith, not feeling. For that means training us to rely on His word, not ours. It's really very simple to understand. It's only hard to accept.

And the Eucharist is the most perfect of all possible training devices. For (1) it does not give us any sight of Him at all, (2) it does not usually give us any feeling of Him at all, (3) and yet it gives us all of Him, His full presence, (4) which is known by faith alone. We long for joy, and He tells us that He *is* our joy, and that He will be in us Himself, not that He *gives* us joy. (Jn. 15:11) He is not a means, and our joy is not the end. That is idolatry. *He* is the end.

Heaven cannot admit any idolatry into its precincts. So He has to wean us from our experience-addiction and direct all our faith and love to Him, not to ourselves. Christ *is* our joy, and we have Him, really present, always (Matthew 28:20); and therefore we have joy, even when we do not feel it. We need nothing more than Christ. We do not need Christ plus joy, or Christ plus experience; we need only Christ. But we also need one more thing: we need *to know* that we need only Christ.

We usually think that there is something wrong with us when the Eucharist does not register on our feelings. No; it does not register not because we are making a mistake but because *God* is *not* making a mistake. He is training us in faith, taking His fatherly hand off our two-wheeler bike so that we can learn to move ahead on the wheels of faith rather than on the helping hand of feelings. He knows all our weaknesses, so He knows our addiction to feelings, and mercifully refuses to satisfy it. He will not give us a spiritual sweet tooth.

There is a famous saying—I think it is from the Chinese Christian writer Watchman Nee—about faith and feeling. Fact, Faith, and Feeling are three men walking on a wall. Fact goes first, Faith second, and Feeling third. As long as Faith keeps his eyes ahead on Fact, all three stay on the wall and make progress. But as soon as Faith takes his eyes off Fact and turns around to see how Feeling is doing, Faith falls off the wall, and Feeling follows, while Fact walks on. The point is obvious: the object of our faith is not feeling but fact, not subjective experience but objective truth.

This is also the key to the mysterious longing, the *"Sehnsucht,"* that C.S. Lewis so powerfully articulates: it is a longing for Christ, for the One who is to be found in the Eucharist. We "hunt his face" (to quote James Taylor's haunting line from "New Hymn") everywhere, for "the heart is a lonely hunter." But our hearts are restless until they rest in Him, and they will wholly rest in Him only when both parts of our blessedness, objective and subjective, are fulfilled, in Heaven.

Until then, as C.S. Lewis says, quoting George Macdonald, the only thing we can do if we are haunted by the smell of unseen roses, is to work. The longing will not come back if we aim at it, if we make an idol of it. The fire will blaze only if we "bank it down with the unlikely fuel of dogma and ethics," faith and works, "trust and obey" (the 1921 hymn title of Rev. J.H. Sammis).

This "trust and obey" applies especially to the

Eucharist. He said, "Take and eat," not "Take and feel." Nor did He say, "Take and understand." He said, "This is my Body," not "This is My mind." Socrates and Solomon and Aquinas and Buddha left us their minds, but Christ left us His body.

If the Incarnation is, as Kierkegaard called it, "the absolute paradox," then the Eucharist is the absolute paradox squared. We need this: an object that reason and understanding cannot attain, any more than sight or feeling can, so that pure faith can say, in Thomas Aquinas's words, "Sight, taste, and touch in Thee are each deceived. / The ear alone most safely is believed. / I believe all the Son of God has spoken./ Than Truth's own word there is no truer token." ("*Adoro Te Devote*") Or, putting the same principle into Southern Baptist language, "God said it, I believe it, and that settles it."

A true incident: a priest had once brought the Eucharist to a bedridden hospital patient, as he had done thousands of times, and sensed nothing unusual about it. But a few days later his pastor asked him what had happened in that hospital room on that day. "Nothing, Father. Why?" "Because I was told just today that a few minutes before you came in, that woman was told by her doctor that her tests were final, and fatal, and that they were sending her home to die. She was in despair. "Then," she said, "a minute later Jesus Christ came into my room and into my body and into my soul, and now the darkness is all gone and everything is light."

When we get Feeling off the throne, God can come in and give us gifts, both of faith and even of feeling, that we could never give ourselves. But He does it in His time schedule, not ours. He's a lover, not a train.

I love the Eucharist because it does *not* appeal to my sight, my reason, or my feelings—that is, to my flesh (fallen human nature, in all its parts). Only thus can it give me true blessedness.

* * * * *

Let's summarize the essential diagnosis again, boiled down to its essence. There are two parts to blessedness. One part is happiness, in the modern, subjective sense of the word—the experience. The other part is the real presence of the real object that causes the experience. That objective part is Christ Himself, and He makes Himself fully present to us in this life in the Eucharist. The subjective half is not full until the next life, because we are not ready for it yet.

In light of this diagnosis, our prescription logically follows: ignore the subjective part, which simply cannot be "jump-started" in this life, and focus on the objective part, which is fully present and working. That is the only way to train the subjective part. Forget yourself and you will be fulfilled; die to yourself and you will live. Don't put your faith in faith; put all your faith in Christ alone. If you do that, you will have no room left for faith in faith, no room left for idolatry. And then it will be safe for God to give you gifts. Sweet desserts are safe only when they are not the main meal.

This is true for a local church, for a parish, as well as for an individual. The difference between a parish's faith in, and focus on, the Real Presence of Christ Himself, and its focus on themselves, or on "community" instead—that is, on *our* presence instead of His—is the explanation of the difference between the parish that is alive and the parish that is half-dead.

I often wondered at the *cause* of those dreary, faithless Modernist parishes and "Catholic" colleges whose religion is all vague, abstract slogans and ideologies ("compassion," "peace and justice," "sharing and caring," "celebrating community," etc.). They always focus on *what we do*, both in the liturgy and in the world, instead of what God does. The faith in the Real Presence is so missing that they don't even know what's missing. They're so dead that they don't know they're dead. Who but dead souls could care about what's left when Jesus's real presence is gone? Why bother playing with toy tigers? Nietzsche said, "When God is dead, the churches become His tombs." Nietzsche must have visited churches like that.

That's why Modernists don't build cathedrals to worship in, but buildings that look like schools or offices. It's not just a question of aesthetic taste, but of faith. Only faith in the Real Presence in the Eucharist built those cathedrals. They were not built for man but for God, to give God Incarnate a fitting reception, to undo the scandal of "no room in the inn" as extravagantly as possible. They were supreme extravagance. They were the woman's alabaster box broken over Christ's feet. (Mt. 26:7; Lk. 7:37)

Cathedrals are boudoirs for trysts with God, passion palaces where two passions meet, love responding to Love, man's astonished love of Christ responding to Christ's astonishing love of man. He came all the way down from Heaven to the Cross just to love and save us; so we went up into the heavens as much as medieval technology allowed (and more!) in building cathedrals to show to the world the incomparable beauty of His divinity which He concealed under the appearances of a crucified criminal, and then the incomparable beauty of His humanity which He concealed under the appearances of a humble little circle of unleavened bread.

Peter's spontaneous response to the Transfiguration vision of Christ's glory on the mountaintop was, "Lord, let us build three booths here." (Mt. 17:4) It was a childish thing to say. But it was also childlike, and his childlike wish was fulfilled beyond his wildest dreams 1000 years later when Christendom caught the same vision of the shocking beauty of Jesus Christ that Peter caught on the mountaintop, and built many more than three "booths," rather large ones, at Notre Dame, at Chartres, at Westminster, at Cologne . . .

Now comes the final shock: you are that cathedral.

Man is a cathedral, and God is its builder. You are even more miraculously beautiful than the cathedrals. You are supernaturally beautiful, and for the same reason the cathedrals are: because you are designed to house the holy God in the body, in matter, time, and space. "Do you not know? Your body is the temple of the Holy Spirit!" (I Cor. 6:19)

What the angel told Mary would come true in her womb, also comes true in our souls: "The Holy Spirit will come upon you, and the power of the Most High will overshadow you; therefore the child to be born of you will be called holy, the Son of God." (Luke 1:35) This happens to us in baptism. Jesus is born in us when we are "born again" in Him. This is the supreme beauty and glory of man.

Just as the cathedrals are the most perfect buildings in human history, man's body is the most perfect organization of matter in the history of the universe. For what? To honor God. This is the glory of man: that he is the glory of God. St. Ignatius of Loyola said, "the glory of God is a man fully alive." He did not mean some vague humanism; he meant Christ. We are fully alive only when we are "born again" with Christ's life. We are fully alive only when we can say, with St. Paul, "I live; nevertheless not I, but Christ lives in me." (Gal. 2:20) We are fully alive only when we are fully dead: "For you have died, and your life is hid with Christ in God." (Col. 3:3)

(By the way, it is far better to speak of "the glory of man" than "the dignity of man." "Dignity" is such a grey, respectable, stuffy, self-conscious, strutting kind of word; while "glory" is a wild, poetic, crazy, fiery, out-flinging kind of word, full of bright blues and flaming yellows. "Dignity" is an owlish word; "glory" is an eagle-ish word. Look what the Church has instinctively chosen to decorate the monstrance holding the Eucharist: not a cage or a safe but a sunburst, a fire. A perfect physical symbol for the state of soul we called "Jesus-shock.")

* * * * *

We pointed out many examples in the Gospels of "Jesus-shock" (pp. 71–97), and we explained their cause as His Real Presence—a presence which persists in the Eucharist. One example of "Jesus-shock" in the Gospels is privileged, because it is explicitly about the Eucharist. That is John 6.

Here, the shock comes from His future promise, not just from the present. Jesus is already present in the flesh (which is shocking enough), but He promises that He will do something even more shocking: He will give them His flesh to eat.

No interpretation of this passage, whether

Catholic or Protestant, "gets the point" of it, and the shock of it, if it fails to perceive Jesus's deliberate juxtaposition of the two meanings of this shocking phrase "eat My flesh and drink My blood." They are, of course, the two historical occurrences of Jesus actually giving us His flesh to eat, namely the Cross and the Eucharist. On the Cross, we did not literally "eat" and "drink" His flesh and blood, but we received it physically and literally into our world, and only because of this did we receive our only hope, our only salvation. In the Eucharist, He did not literally bleed and die again—the one sacrifice of the Cross, given "once and for all" (Heb. 10:10) and "finished" (Jn. 19:30), is not re-sacrificed but re-offered "in an unbloody manner." (*Catechism of the Catholic Church* 1367; Council of Trent (1562): DS 1743; cf. *Heb.* 9:14, 27) But there we do literally eat and drink His body and blood.

He is really present, fully present, "body and blood, soul and divinity," in both events. Both events are literal. But half of each event is physical and the other half is not. On the Cross, His body is given physically and chemically, but we do not receive it physically and chemically, into our mouths. In the Eucharist, His giving of Himself is no longer physical and chemical (chemical analysis of the consecrated Host reveals only the appearances of bread, and He does not physically die again), but our receiving of Him is physical and chemical.

Let's see what new gems we can find in this old, familiar mine shaft of John 6. It yields inexhaustible gems because it is inexhaustibly deep. For this mine shaft goes down into the Mind of God.

> The Jews then murmured at him, because he said, "I am the bread which came down from heaven." They said, "Is this not Jesus, the son of Joseph, whose father and mother we know? How does he now say, 'I have come down from heaven'?" Jesus answered them . . . "I am the bread of life. Your fathers ate the manna in the wilderness, and they died. This is the bread which comes down from heaven, that a man may eat of it and not die. I am the living bread which came down from heaven; if any one eats of this bread, he will live for ever; and the bread which I shall give for the life of the world is my flesh." The Jews then disputed among themselves, saying, "How can this man give us his flesh to eat?" So Jesus said to them, "Truly, truly I say to you, unless you eat the flesh of the Son of man and drink his blood, you have no life in you; he who eats my

flesh and drinks my blood has eternal life, and I will raise him up at the last day. For my flesh is food indeed, and my blood is drink indeed . . . " Many of his disciples, when they heard it, said, "This is a hard saying; who can listen to it?" . . . After this many of his disciples drew back and no longer went about with him. Jesus said to the twelve, "Will you also go away?" Simon Peter answered him, "Lord, to whom shall we go? You have the words of everlasting life." (John 6:41–68)

It is probably impossible for us to realize how shocking Jesus's words were when first uttered— not only because they have become familiar but also because we are not Jews, for whom Mosaic law, God's own law, strictly forbade them ever to eat human flesh or to drink any blood at all. God had told them: "I will set my face against that person who eats blood, and will cut him off from among his people. For the life of the flesh is in the blood; and I have given it for you upon the altar to make atonement for your souls; for it is the blood that makes atonement, by reason of the life." (Leviticus 17: 10–11) The point of the Mosaic liturgical taboo was to keep God's Chosen People virginally pure for Him, pure of animal blood so that they could receive divine blood.

Jesus' words shock because they bear a striking resemblance to the cannibalism, vampirism, and human sacrifice of the liturgies of Hell, celebrated in Aztec Mexico and in the Valley of Gehenna in ancient Canaan. Of course this is putting it exactly backwards: Christ's liturgy was not a purified imitation of Hell's, but Hell's was a perverse imitation of Christ's.

The passage I quoted from John 6 immediately follows the miracle of the multiplication of the loaves and fishes to feed 5000 people. After that sign, Jesus tells the people what it signified. It is Himself. It is not some good but abstract ideal like "sharing and caring," or generosity, or compassion. It is His own body. "*I am* the bread of life."

We have to eat Him to become Him, because "*Man ist was er isst*" ("you are what you eat"). We eat the bread that perishes (vs. 27), and we perish. We eat the Imperishable Man, and become imperishable.

We ask wrongly if we ask what the "point" of the bread is (vs. 33). It's not a point; it's a Person! Jesus, nothing more and nothing less, is what the manna meant (vss. 31–32). He now made manna again, feeding five thousand people, to show them who He was: both the Maker of the sign (the giver of the manna bread) and what the sign signified. He tells them clearly: the manna "came down from Heaven" precisely to signify Himself, who came down from Heaven. And why did He come? To give us the true manna, His flesh, His body.

And why did He do that, why did He give us His body instead of just giving us His mind, His teaching, His truth? So that we could not just know Him and love Him and imitate Him but *eat* Him. And why must we eat Him? So that we can *be* Him. For it is not said that "you *are* what you know" or "you *are* what you imitate" but it is said that "You *are* what you eat." Our destiny is Christification, divinization, *theosis*, as the Eastern Orthodox call it, in Greek. (No, it's not pagan Greek mysticism, it's in the Bible: II Peter 1:4.)

When Jesus uttered these shocking words, many left him. (Jn. 6:60) Protestants follow this crowd, but Peter and his successors remained faithful—to Christ and to this saying of His (vss. 66–68), the saying that forever after, down through the ages, would always be a touchstone for Catholic orthodoxy. The Petrine office (later called the "papacy") and the doctrine of the Eucharist are always found together throughout church history. Whoever rejects the one, always eventually rejects the other. For they are similar scandals of particularity and concreteness.

It is not a question merely of the correct doctrine about the Eucharist, and it is not merely a question of the correct doctrine about the authority of Peter and his successors. It is a question of fidelity to Christ. The Pope is the vicar *of Christ*, and the Eucharist *is* Christ.

If the popes are *not* the vicars of Christ and the inheritors of His promises to Peter of the keys to the Kingdom of Heaven, binding and loosing with Heavenly authority; if sinful Peter and his sinful successors are *not* the divinely appointed rock on which He founded His Church, and forever unconquerable even by the very powers of death and Hell (Mt. 16:13–19); then the popes who claim these promises are false prophets and blasphemous pretenders, and ecumenically minded Protestants who respect the Catholic Church are less logically consistent, though more charitable, than Fundamentalist fulminators who denounce her.

In a precisely parallel way, if the Eucharist is *not* Christ Himself, then Catholics are the most outrageously egregious, perniciously perfidious, idiotically idolatrous, and nefariously necrophiliac blasphemers in history when they bow to bread as if it were God. (No, they don't bow to bread. That's not bread. It only looks like bread. That's God, even though it doesn't look like God.)

There is another scandal that fits this same pattern of either-or extremes: Christ Himself. If He is not God incarnate, He is literally the worst, most dangerous, most evil man who ever lived. A mere man who claims to be God and wants you to give him your soul, to put all your faith, all your hope, and all your love in him—if he is not God incarnate, he is the Devil incarnate. There is no wiggle room here. There is no mushy middle. The laws of logic make it either/or. It's either true or false. Once the claim is staked, there simply is no third option, ever, anywhere. To be or not to be: that is the question. His claim to be God is the sword that divides all of time and history into two halves, B.C. vs. A.D., and divides the population of the world into two halves, like a junction on a train track. And both tracks go to eternity.

The other Biblical character with the same name as Jesus also staked such a claim and forced his people (the same people, God's chosen ones, His collective prophet to the world) to make the same absolute choice for or against. His name was

Joshua, and his words "Choose ye this day whom ye will serve!" (Joshua 24:15) have continued to ring down through the centuries while the echoes of all the attempts to construct a mushy middle have died out.

I know there have been many other "takes" on Jesus, many alternative Christianities, many alternative Christologies, many attempts to construct a mushy middle and escape this terrifying either/or. It does not matter what I think of these alternatives. It matters what Christ thinks of them. And the Gospels are painfully clear about that.

Christ's Incarnation was an act of war. Christ's establishing the Eucharist was an act of war. Christ's giving Peter the keys to His kingdom was an act of war. And He knew it. He said it. He said that He came to divide the world, not to unite it. (Mt. 10:34) Our whole modern secularist mentality is wrong. We are not at peace, we are at war. Woe to those "who say peace, peace when there is no peace." (Jer. 6:14) The war is not with flesh and blood. It is worse than that. It is with demons. (Eph. 6:12) If that is not true, the Bible is a tissue of lies and myths, like Greek mythology, no matter how much beauty and morality peek through.

The word "Eucharist" or "Eucharistic" sounds

somehow vaguely "churchy": nice, safe, polite, proper, reserved, archaic, arcane, technical, and "theological." But the Eucharist is not safe. It is dangerous. It can kill you. Cf. I Corinthians 11:27–30.

The Eucharist is a sword. It is pointed at your heart. This is not a clever ploy of mine, an image I invented; it is pure scriptural logic. For the Eucharist is Christ, and Christ is the Word of God, and the Word of God is a sword. (Hebrews 4:12) A=B=C=D.

Christ's "This is My Body, given up for you" is one side in the war. The other side, the side He came to earth to defeat and to free us from, also says "This is my body," but means exactly the opposite thing by it: not the self-sacrifice of the martyr but the arrogant pride of the egotist. The spirit of Antichrist says, through his deluded slaves who think they are asserting their freedom, "This is *my* body, not Yours. You did not create me. You have no rights over me. I am the master of my fate. I am the captain of my soul. When I die, I will not repent in shame but I will hold my head erect and sing 'I did it my way' as I enter the realm of my chosen lord and model, Satan, who did exactly that same thing many eons ago. This is *my* body, and therefore I will fornicate, contracept, sodomize, or commit suicide as I choose. I am the master of my fate, I am the captain of my soul. I will do whatever *I* please with my body because it is mine, not Yours. In fact, the tiny child I carry in my womb is also mine, not Yours. She is not even her own. She is mine. She is *my* body. Therefore I will kill her, because I am her God, and You are not." You see, abortion is the Antichrist's demonic parody of the Eucharist. That is why it uses the same holy words, "This is my body," with the blasphemously opposite meaning.

Part Five: What Do We Do Now?

"WHAT SHALL WE SAY then to these things?"
(Rom. 8: 31) What shall we do about it? How can
we fight the good fight? "What can we do, to do
the works of God?" That was precisely the question
Christ was asked in John 6:28. And His answer
was that the first work of God is to believe in Him.
(Jn. 6:29)

Then, if we believe in Him, we will fall down
and adore Him.

Where? Why, where He is, of course.

And where is He? In many places, and in many
ways—in human hearts, and in the poor, and in the
good social causes that fight for the good in a
world full of evil, and in the living word of scripture. But above all, in the Eucharist.

Why "above all" there? Because there alone He
is fully, literally, totally, and perfectly present and
therefore to be adored. We do not adore the poor,

or the saints, or the Bible, even though He is present there too. For He is not present there as He is in the Eucharist. The Church calls it "the source and summit of the Christian life." (*Catechism of the Catholic Church* 1324; *Lumen Gentium* 11)

Adoring God is the first and greatest commandment. And Christ is God. Therefore adoring Christ is the first and greatest commandment, our Commander's first command for spiritual battle. And He is fully present to be adored only in the Eucharist. Therefore Eucharistic adoration is the foundation for all our other acts of holy warfare.

What is the holy war about? Not just rights, or even righteousness, but salvation. And not just temporal bodies but eternal souls. The war is about salvation vs. damnation, Heaven vs. Hell. Please don't call that crude fundamentalism, because that comes from Jesus, not from me.

And it's about you. What's at stake in this war is whether you will go to Heaven or not, and then whether you will help other people to go to Heaven or not. The war begins and ends at your back door, just as the great, worldwide War of the Ring began and ended at the very door of Bag End, Frodo's hobbit-hovel, in the plot of the greatest book of the 20th century.

So please be alone with Christ now, frequently, before the Eucharist. This is one of the most practical things you can possibly do. For there will come a day, sooner than you wish, when you will be alone with Him and unable to return to your friends or your family or your home or the pleasures of the world, ever again. You will be alone with Christ at the border of eternity. Why wait until that momentous moment to be alone with Him? Why not *practice*?

The supreme practice is communal: the Mass. Just as Heaven is communal (scripture never describes Heaven as private mystical experience, but always as public liturgy), so is earth. Those cathedrals were built not only to house the Eucharist for private adoration, but above all for the public celebration of the Mass, the liturgy, the "*opus dei*," the work of God, the greatest event in history made really present again and again to every time and place. If the Eucharist is the Incarnation squared, the Mass is the Incarnation cubed.

To many people, "liturgy" and "liturgical" sounds "churchy," and "churchy" sounds vaguely sweet and sleepy. Liturgical terms like "Paschal mystery" and "Eucharistic sign" sound remote and removed from real life. Many people on the "right" dislike the subject of liturgy because it feels so soft and squooshy compared to clear, hard, solid creeds and commandments, the other two dimensions of the Catholic faith. Others, on the "left," get the same feeling of softness when they think of liturgy, but they *like* it, especially compared to creeds and commandments. They think liturgy leaves them more "free" and "creative" than creeds and commandments. They often say nice, soft, squooshy things like "liturgy celebrates community"—meaning themselves.

Both sides are wrong. Liturgy is not soft and squooshy, unless Christ is. It is not a humanly invented work of creative art, either ancient or modern. It is neither a delicate, ornate, out-of-date antique nor a practical, up-to-date piece of contemporary "relevance" (i.e. irrelevance). It is hard. It is objectively real. It is not some *thing* at all; it is *someone.* It is Jesus. "It is the mystery of Christ that the Church proclaims and celebrates in her liturgy" (*Catechism of the Catholic Church* 1068). And when this is understood, it administers "Jesus-shock."

For Christ is not dead but alive in the liturgy. He is not just the *object* of our faith and devotion, our memory and love; He is *the acting subject.*

("Look out! He's alive!") He actually *does things to us* in His sacraments. (That's why He instituted them!) Christ is not merely remembered, like a dead man, but encountered, "alive and kicking" like a stallion. "It is always shocking to meet life when we thought we were alone . . . when the [fishing] line pulls at your hand, when something breathes beside you in the darkness . . . 'Look out,' we cry, 'it's alive!'" (C.S. Lewis, *Miracles,* ch. 11) And *that* is what happens in all seven of the Church's sacraments.

And the thing He does is, in one word, salvation. ("The Church celebrates in her liturgy above all . . . the work of our salvation." *Catechism of the Cahtolic Church* 1067) The sacraments, and above all the Mass, not only *recall* the events that saved us but it *actualizes* them, it makes them really present when it makes Christ really present. For that's what He came for, and that's what He does when He comes: He saves us.

Going to Mass and receiving Holy Communion is a tryst with our divine lover. Nothing could possibly be less vague and abstract and safe and squooshy. Nothing could possibly be less boring. For nothing is less safe and soft and squooshy and boring than Jesus Christ. He is not a ghost;

when you touch Him, you touch iron and fire. It is you who are the ghost. Touching Him is the way to become solid.

This is the reason all Protestants should become Catholics: because only there can they fulfill their deepest and most right and righteous longing as good Protestants: to feed on Christ's most solid food, Himself. When a Jew becomes a Christian, he rightly says, "I have become more Jewish, not less. I am now a completed Jew. I have fulfilled my Law and Prophets. I have found my Messiah." And when an Evangelical Protestant becomes a Catholic, he rightly says, "I have fulfilled my Evangelicalism. I have become more Evangelical, not less. I have found the depth and center of the *Evangelium*, the Good News. I feared the Church as an idol, a distraction from Christ, but I have found that it is more fully Christic and Christocentric than anything else in the world."

But Protestants won't become Catholics until Catholics do! I've been preaching mainly to Protestants in this section; let me now preach to Catholics.

Everyone knows the Church is in crisis. In every significant respect, her numbers have been more than cut in half in Europe and North

America. The names are still on the baptismal rolls, but names don't believe, hope, love, worship, and become saints; people do. Fifty years ago, 75 percent went to Sunday Mass; now it's 25 percent. That's America; numbers in Western Europe are far lower. The numbers for Confession are even starker. The last generation's theological knowledge has been almost abolished: college graduates know less theology today than fifth graders knew fifty years ago. Literally. I know. I teach them. I do not exaggerate. Not one in fifty Catholic college students has ever even heard that Christ is one person with two natures, or that the Trinity means that God is one in nature and three in persons. Most are amazed that anyone ever tried to prove the existence of God by philosophical reasoning. Worst of all, when asked why they expect God to accept them into Heaven when they die, only one in twenty even mention Jesus Christ. (This is not an estimate. This is a statistic, based on hundreds of questionnaires.) Can there be any possible educational scandal worse than that?

And the Church's *moral* teaching is in even worse shape. If it has anything to do with sexuality, it is simply not preached, or it is misunderstood, or it is ignored, with embarrassment, or it is simply rejected and even sneered at, with the exception of abortion (because that's like racism: it's so obviously wrong that you don't have to be a Catholic to see it). For the last forty years I have not heard a single homily that labeled any sexual sin a sin at all. Only the Church's social morality is preached, and even that only very selectively. (How many have ever heard of the principle of subsidiarity? It is anathema to Socialists and Democrats, so it is not preached.)

What is the root of the crisis of faith? What is the taproot of all the dullness and ineffectiveness of most parishes, clergy, laity, homilies, music, catechesis, and all the nice, fussy, busy, Martha-like programs and activities? Why have Evangelical, Fundamentalist, nondenominational, and Pentecostal churches been so much more successful than Catholics, in quantity of converts and in intensity of commitment, throughout the Western Hemisphere for the past fifty years? Why would Catholics, who are in possession of the fullness of the Faith, exchange it for a faith that is only partial? Why swap a cathedral for a ranch house?

It is not usually outright heresy or apostasy. It is not primarily because of a disbelief in or disaffection for any of the positive, distinctively

Catholic things that Protestants lack—history, tradition, popes, saints, sacraments, etc. Attacks on these things come later, after the initial choice; they do not usually motivate the choice.

It is not even primarily because of the post-Vatican II apostasy (no nicer word will do) in catechesis, the rejection of solid, full texts like the Baltimore Catechism or the St. Joseph Catechism and the substitution of those stunningly stupid, impossibly insipid CCD texts from Benziger and Sadlier that dress up vacuity and vagueness in the prose of pop-psychology platitudes and bureaucratic banalities. Jesus tells us His reaction to them in a strikingly concrete verb in Rev. 3:16. Look it up. Read His whole letter, substituting "Europe and America" for "Laodicea." Put the two things side by side. See how they fit.

But even such catastrophically boring catechesis (so boring that it is almost interesting, like a pile of mud a hundred feet high) is the result, not the cause; the symptom, not the disease.

Even the heresies of liberal or modernist theology, the denial of the supernatural (which is never honestly argued, usually just subtly, sophisticatedly, and sophistically taken for granted) is not the very first and deepest infidelity, because the orthodox *theology* that Modernism rejected was not the very first and deepest fidelity. The primary object of faith, says St. Thomas, is not the articles of the creeds, but Christ Himself; not propositions but the Person who is presented by the propositions. The crisis in the Church today is a crisis of Christlessness.

Among the sheep, it is simply a crisis of not being fed. But among the shepherds, it is the more terrible crisis of a fear of feeding. By the shepherds I do not mean the Pope and the average, hard-working, pious parish priest but the "intellectuals," the writers of CCD texts and the heads of pastoral institutes and the theology teachers and the ex-nuns (I have learned never to trust an ex-nun) and many of the pastors and rectors and bishops (yes, bishops; Judas Iscariot was a bishop) who were trained in the sixties and seventies and eighties. The teachers are terrified of the thought that they might actually have something divine to teach. They are terrified of dogma, of Tradition, of Divine Revelation, of Divine Law, of authority, of "Thus says the Lord."

But the Lord is Christ. So the crisis is not just Christlessness but Christophobia.

You can understand why. You can even sympathize with them. For this soul food to which they are anorexic is alive and dangerous. It's "Christ the tiger," not Christ the kitten. Get close to Him and you feel blood, and splinters. You see a fire blazing. You hear the rattle of dry bones coming to life, and the shouts of joy and glory and battle that ring through the Psalms and the great old Protestant hymns. It's not *polite*. It's much more comfortable to see Jesus as a pop psychologist and the Church as Mister Roger's Neighborhood.

How do we get the fire back? There is no gimmick. We just (1) believe everything God has told us through Church and Scripture, and (2) respond with adoration. And then everything else that is necessary will follow—as it did for Mary, for whom there was "only one thing needful," and as it did for all the saints, and as it does for Mother Teresa's Missionaries of Charity, who are simply the holiest and happiest people in this entire world.

Adoration means especially Eucharistic adoration. In that silence there is a power greater than a thousand nuclear bombs, greater than the sun, greater than the Big Bang. It is the power of God, released when the atom of the Trinity was split on the Cross and the explosion of redeeming blood came out. In Eucharistic adoration we touch this power, which is the root of everything, for it is Christ the *Pantocrator*. We touch the candle of our souls to the fire of His passion, His passion for souls, and we catch that flame.

But we must do this for His sake, not for our sakes, and not even for the sake of revival in the Church. In fact, our motive should not even be the salvation of the world first of all, but for Him first of all. He is not a means to any end; He is the end. He must be adored for His own sake, because of what He is. He commands us to-adore-Him-for-His-own-sake, not to-adore-him-for-our-sake; but He commands this for our sake, not for His own sake, since He does not need us but we need Him. His glory is to be our concern; our glory is His concern. That is what love is: a holy Exchange.

When we enter that holy Exchange we enter the very life of the eternal Trinity. And God will never, never, never, never give up on us until we do.

Part Six: Seven Postscripts

1. "JESUS-SHOCK" IS NOT necessarily emotional. It's not a "high." It's not detectable by heavy breathing. In fact, it's detectable when you *stop* breathing for a moment. At the moment of the Consecration, at the moment of your reception of Communion, you do not breathe normally. You stop. Time stops. Time stops when He comes because Time is one of His servants, and the King's servants do not walk but bow when the King comes into the room.

This is not emotional because it is more, not less, than an emotion.

2. The subtler, deeper, less emotional and more constant sense of His Real Presence is much more precious and more crucial to us than the initial Jesus-shock, and it is the purpose and end to which Jesus-shock is designed to lead. Jesus-shock is like falling in love. It is not designed for itself, but for marriage.

3. The "Christocentrism" of this book, the "Jesus only" point of this book, is meant to contrast to all other centers, all idols, all additions and subtractions and emendations and substitutions and dilutions of Jesus. But it is not meant to contrast to the other two divine Persons. Jesus's whole point is to point to the Father. He comes into the world to do the Father's will, not His own (Jn. 4:34; 5:30) and to give us the Father's mind and teaching, not His own. (Jn. 7:16) He says, "He who has seen me has seen the Father. (Jn. 14:9) For "I and my Father are one." (Jn. 10:30) He also sends the Spirit to be more perfectly with us, more intimately in us, than He Himself was. (John 16:7) There is never any rivalry, any either/or, in the Trinity. Christocentrism and theocentrism are rivals only for heretics.

4. Therefore "Jesus-shock" leads to charismatic Christianity, Spirit-filled Christianity, Pentecostal Christianity. After all, only the Holy Spirit creates Jesus-shock. And as the Holy Spirit is wholly for Christ, Christ is wholly for the Holy Spirit. He came to give us the Spirit. Jesus is presented in all four Gospels, in contrast to John the Baptist, as the one who will baptize with the Holy Spirit and with

fire, not only with water. Water baptism is the beginning, as water is the foundational food for all living things. But spirit baptism, fire-baptism, is the end. We begin as wet marshes but we are meant to catch fire.

The Holy Spirit gives us an even greater intimacy with God. The Father is God outside us, the Son is God beside us, and the Spirit is God inside us.

The Spirit is the fire; the Church is the fireplace. Tragically, these two things are separated in our world. Most of institutional Christianity is a fireplace without much of a fire; and most of Pentecostal or charismatic Christianity is a fire without much of a fireplace. The first is a body without a soul; the other is a soul without a body. Neither is fully human, neither is the full Christ.

When the two are perfectly united, the Church will win the world again.

5. Christocentrism displaces nothing except all other *centers*. It does not displace anything else but idolatries. It displaces only displacements. It displaces the wrong placement of other things, the placing of them at the center. But it does not displace any of these other things. If we seek His

kingdom first, all other things will be added to us. (Mt. 6:33) "Jesus only" means not "Jesus versus everything" but "Jesus as Lord of everything, Jesus as the center of everything, Jesus as the Lover and Designer and Creator and Redeemer and Glorifier of everything." Grace perfects nature. The "only" of "Jesus only" is the catholic, universal, inclusive both/and "only," not the puritan, fundamentalist, exclusive, either/or "only."

"Christ" means the whole Christ, Head and Body. And His Body is us and our whole world. We humanize the world, as our larger body, or the extension of our body; and He divinizes us, and makes us part of His larger Body; and thus through us He makes the whole world part of His Body. (See Teilhard de Chardin's *The Divine Milieu* on this. It's really very, very profound. Flaky, airy, liberal Catholics love his *The Phenomenon of Man*, but many solid, orthodox, conservative Catholics like Henri de Lubac and Flannery O'Connor love *The Divine Milieu*.)

6. Christocentrism is not a theory or a theology but a practice. It was perfectly expressed by St. Thomas Aquinas when Christ asked him, from the crucifix (according to sworn testimony from his friend and

confessor Brother Reginald), "You have written well of me, Thomas; what will you have as your reward?" (He asks the same thing of all of us: "What do you want?" This was Jesus's very first question in John's Gospel [1:38]. Christocentrism is St. Thomas's perfect reply: "Only Thyself, Lord.")

7. Christocentrism means that Christ is the Golden Key that opens all doors. What are some of these doors? Ecumenism, education, fear, boredom, death, hermeneutics, eschatology, epistemology, family. There are dozens of doors, and Christ is the one skeleton key that opens them all. How does this work? That question will take another whole book to answer.

Index

Biblical References

10 BOOKS
THAT WILL CHANGE YOUR LIFE!

1. *The Philosophy of Jesus* by Peter Kreeft

2. *An Ocean Full of Angels* by Peter Kreeft

3. *Lord of the World* by Robert Hugh Benson

4. *The Latin Letters of C.S. Lewis* by C.S. Lewis & St. Giovanni Calabria

5. *Morality: The Catholic View* by Servais Pinckaers, O.P.

6. *What Catholics Believe* by Josef Pieper & Heinz Raskop

7. *The John Paul II LifeGuide: Words to Live By* by John Paul II

8. *The Christian Idea of Man* by Josef Pieper

9. *Natural Law* by Jacques Maritain

10. *The Last Superstition: A Refutation of the New Atheism* by Edward Feser

We offer a 25% discount to everyone working through **The Dynamic Catholic Institute.** Just go to our website, chose the books you want, and at checkout put the promo code DYNAMIC in the box to receive the 25% discount on the entire order.
-prices above reflect discount-

St. Augustine's Press
online: www.staugustine.net
telephone: (800) 621-2736
promo code: DYNAMIC

NOTES

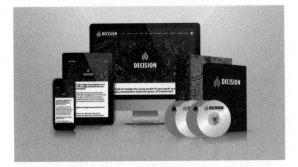

THE
DYNAMIC CATHOLIC
INSTITUTE

[MISSION]

To re-energize the Catholic Church
in America by developing world-class
resources that inspire people to
rediscover the genius of Catholicism.

[VISION]

To be the innovative leader in the
New Evangelization helping Catholics
and their parishes become
the-best-version-of-themselves.

DynamicCatholic.com
Be Bold. Be Catholic.®

The Dynamic Catholic Institute
5081 Olympic Blvd
Erlanger, Kentucky 41018
Phone: 859-980-7900
Email: info@DynamicCatholic.com